PONS

W0074591

MURDER IN THE MOONLIGHT

Mörderische Kurzkrimis

zum Englischlernen

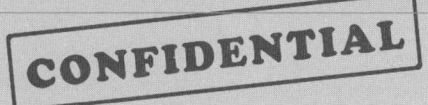

CONFIDENTIAL

von Dominic Butler

PONS GmbH
Stuttgart

PONS
MURDER IN THE MOONLIGHT

Mörderische Kurzkrimis

zum Englischlernen

von Dominic Butler

PONS verpflichtet sich, den Zugriff auf die zu diesem Buch
gehörige Vokabeltrainer-App mindestens bis Ende 2018 zu
gewährleisten. Einen Anspruch der Nutzung darüber hinaus
gibt es nicht.

2. Auflage 2016

© **PONS GmbH, Stuttgart 2015**
Alle Rechte vorbehalten
PONS Online-Wörterbuch: www.pons.eu
E-Mail: info@pons.de

Projektleitung: Francesca Giamboni
Autor: Dominic Butler
Redaktion: Brian Wolfe
Einbandgestaltung: Anne Helbich, Stuttgart
Logoentwurf: Erwin Poell, Heidelberg
Logoüberarbeitung: Sabine Redlin, Ludwigsburg
Layout: Petra Michel, Gestaltung & Typografie, Essen
Satz: Datagroup Int. SRL, Timisoara
Druck: Medienhaus Plump, Rheinbreitbach

ISBN: 978-3-12-562779-6

Dominic Butler

Dominic Butler stammt aus Nordengland. Er ist Englisch-
lehrer und Schriftsteller. Nach seiner Schulzeit, die er an einer
klassischen Grammar School (entspricht dem deutschen
Gymnasium) verbrachte, studierte er Film und Literatur an
der Sheffield Hallam University. Während seiner Studienzeit
arbeitete er in Teilzeit als Gerichtsschreiber am Strafgericht
in Sheffield. Dort erwachte sein Interesse für Kriminalfälle,
die von nun an Thema vieler seiner Kurzgeschichten wurden.
Dominic lebt und arbeitet zurzeit in Italien, wo er Englisch
unterrichtet und gerade seinen ersten Roman beendet, einen
düsteren, jedoch humorvollen Krimi.

EINIGE WORTE VORAB…

Sie lesen gerne Krimis und möchten etwas für Ihr Englisch tun?
Mit diesen spannenden Kriminalgeschichten frischen Sie Ihr Englisch
auf. Die verwendete Sprache passt genau zu Ihrem Lernniveau, so dass
Ihnen das Lesen ganz leicht fällt.

Nicht nur Krimis lesen, sondern auch mehr
über Land und Leute erfahren:
Im Anschluss zu jeder Geschichte finden Sie
wissenswerte Informationen zu den **Schau-
plätzen**, an denen die Geschichten spielen.

Schwierigere Wörter
sind auf jeder Seite
in den **Fußnoten**
übersetzt. Im Anhang
können Sie nochmals
alle Wörter in
einer alphabetischen
Wortliste
nachschlagen.

Wo die einzelnen Schauplätze liegen, können
Sie in der **Weltkarte** auf den Seiten 6 und 7
nachschauen.

Alle Wörter, die in den Fußnoten übersetzt sind, können Sie
mit der **PONS Vokabeltrainer-App** üben. Gehen Sie einfach auf
www.pons.de/kurzkrimis-en und laden Sie die App kostenlos auf Ihr
Smartphone oder Tablet herunter!

INHALTSVERZEICHNIS

– –

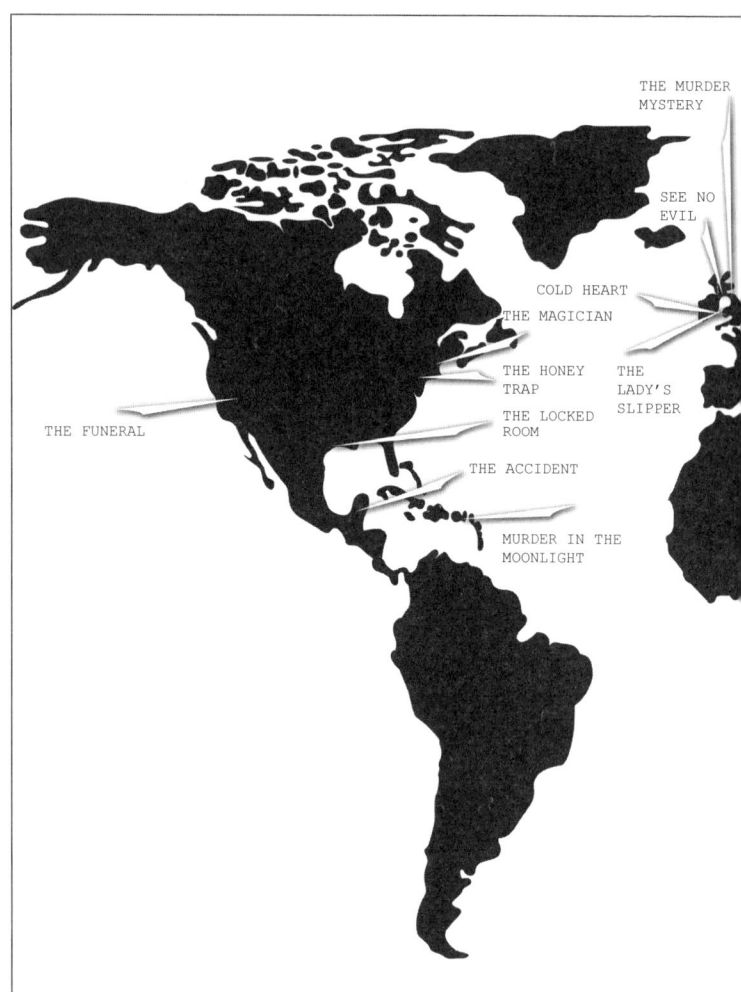

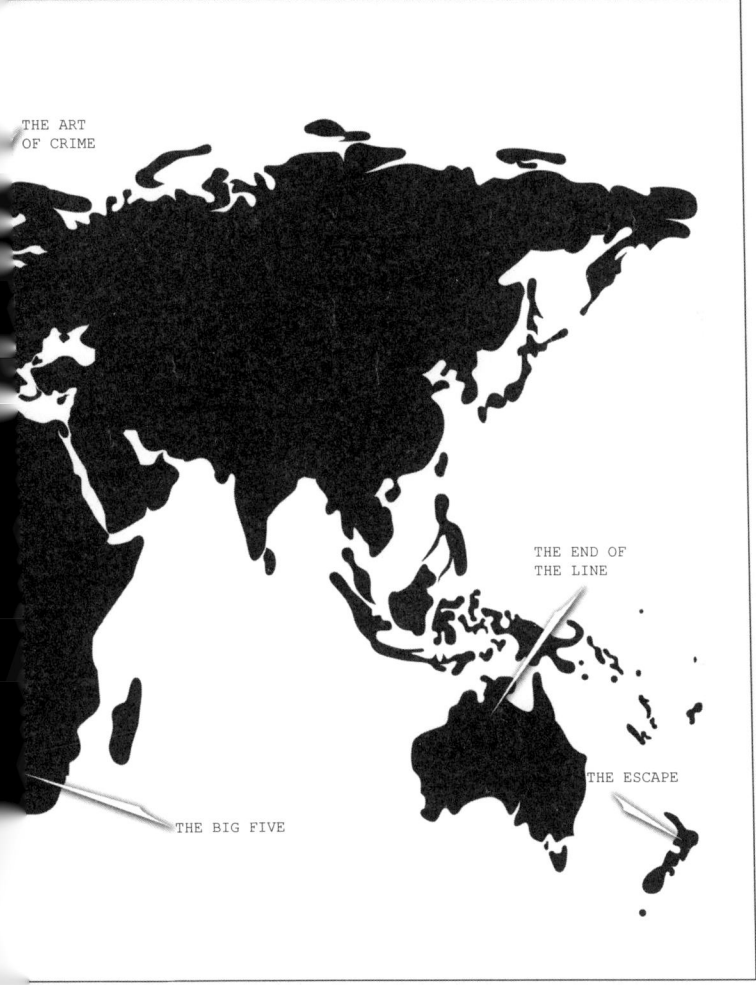

THE ART
OF CRIME

THE END OF
THE LINE

THE ESCAPE

THE BIG FIVE

1.   THE   ACCIDENT

It was an accident.

He was dead, but it was an accident.

Emily felt her legs go weak[1] and she felt like she could not breathe. The tunnels were hot, impossibly hot, and she wanted to take the torch[2] and run along the passages[3] to the entrance and then out into the humid[4] night of the jungle.

But she did not.

Instead she sat down, with her back against the side of the ancient Mayan burial stone[5] and began to cry, the noise echoing[6] around the small room.

Finally the tears stopped and she dried her eyes with the sleeve of her khaki shirt and pushed her brown hair away from her face.

She was not the type of person to cry for no reason, but she knew that what she had done was going to change her life forever.

Yes, it had been an accident, but even if anyone believed her, her career was over, her six years of study a waste of time[7].

And it was all because of him.

She stared[8] for a moment at his body in the dim light from the torch.

Professor Mounier.

---

1   **to feel one's legs go weak** – *weiche Knie bekommen*
2   **torch** – *Taschenlampe*
3   **passage** – *Gang*
4   **humid** – *schwül*
5   **burial stone** – *Grabstein*
6   **to echo** – *widerhallen*
7   **waste of time** – *Zeitverschwendung*
8   **to stare at sth.** – *etw. anstarren*

He looked extremely peaceful. He was not an ugly man, but neither was he handsome. Maybe he had been, twenty years ago, but now he was in his fifties, his stomach was large and his tanned face was covered by his beard.

No, he was not attractive. He was repellent[1]. A serpent, not a man. With hands that never stopped moving, touching, searching and reaching for her.

But not now. No, now he was still, his hands unmoving.

And next to his left eye there was a bloody hole where she had hit him with the small excavation[2] hammer.

For a moment she felt like[3] crying again, but she did not let herself. She had to get to the British embassy[4] before the body was found, explain what had happened, explain that it had not been her fault[5].

Not her fault.

No, it had been his.

For three months she had worked here with him in Belize, excavating a new sequence of tunnels found near to the Caana. It was every young archaeologist's dream. To work with a famous professor like Mounier, to be present at the opening of a new excavation.

But the reality had been different.

She had known that Mounier had been looking for an assistant, and she had gone to see him at his office. At the beginning everything had been pleasant[6]. Yes, they had been flirting a bit, but nothing more than that. But then he had become insistent[7] and talking about his wife was the only way to stop him.

1	**repellent** – *widerwärtig*
2	**excavation** – *Ausgrabung*
3	**to feel like doing sth.** – *Lust haben, etw. zu tun*
4	**embassy** – *Botschaft*
5	**fault** – *Schuld*
6	**pleasant** – *angenehm*
7	**insistent** – *hartnäckig*

Then tonight he had come to the tunnels where she was working alone and she had smelt the alcohol on his breath[1], she had seen the dangerous look in his eyes.

But it was an accident. He had tried to reach for her, and she had told him to stop, but he had not.

So she had stopped him.

She looked at the hammer. Yes, it had not been her fault.

So why should she suffer[2]?

And suddenly she was not thinking about the British embassy anymore. She was thinking that of all the places to hide a body, surely[3] these dark tunnels were the best.

She pushed herself up and looked around.

The body was behind the burial stone, but Mounier's feet could be seen if someone came.

And someone might come[4]. Yes, one of the other assistants, Claire or Stephen, maybe.

Quickly she reached down and grabbed him under his arms, his sweat on her hands, and she pulled him half a metre until the body was hidden.

Then for a moment she looked at the burial stone and contemplated[5] the possibility of placing him beneath it, but no, it was a ridiculous[6] idea. At some point it would be moved again, and then it would be obvious that she had placed him there.

"Think!" she told herself, but all she could do was repeat the words *it was an accident*.

An accident. Yes, that was it. The tunnels were newly excavated and still not completely safe[7]. She could drag[8] the

---

1 **breath –** *Atem*
2 **to suffer –** *leiden*
3 **surely –** *bestimmt*
4 **someone might come –** *jemand könnte kommen*
5 **to contemplate –** *erwägen*
6 **ridiculous –** *absurd*
7 **safe –** *ungefährlich*
8 **to drag –** *schleifen*

body down one of them and then destroy the supports¹ keeping the heavy stone in place. The body would be crushed and the injury from the hammer hidden.

She almost smiled. It was so simple.

Then she heard the sound of footsteps from the entrance and she froze².

"Emily?" a voice said, and then Claire was there, another torch in her hand, a smile on her face. "Are you still here?"

"Yes, nearly finished."

"I'm walking back to the camp in a moment. I can wait for you."

"Oh, no. You should go. Mounier said he wanted to inspect something."

Claire shook her head. "Yeah, right, he just wants to get you in here alone. I hate that man."

Emily saw the hammer on the floor. She tried to smile. "Look, you go, honestly. I want to speak to him too."

Claire stopped smiling, "Wait, you're not? You know? You and him?"

Emily moved in front of the murder weapon. She vigorously³ shook her head. "God, no!"

Claire laughed. "Good! Okay, well. If he tries to touch you, give him a slap⁴. See you later."

And then Emily was alone again. She took a deep breath of the warm air and quickly picked up the hammer and put it in her pocket.

She had to be quick now.

Which was the best tunnel to leave the body in? The east passage was easier to get to, but the west passage was less

---

1   **support** – *Stütze*
2   **to freeze** – *erstarren*
3   **vigorously** – *energisch*
4   **to give sb. a slap** – *jdm. eine Ohrfeige geben*

secure[1]. She could easily break one or two of the supports, and the stone would collapse[2].

Yes, the west.

This time she took hold of Mounier by his feet and began to drag him further into the tunnel, the torch in her mouth.

For ten minutes she dragged him, and when, finally, they were at the less secure area, she stopped, sweat covering her entire body, and looked around.

It was perfect.

A few metres in front of her there were two vertical[3] supports and next to them was a sign that said no one should enter.

She could move the body there and then weaken[4] the supports.

No.

If she did that, the whole structure could collapse on top of her.

"Think!"

Then in the shadow of the tunnel she saw a coil of rope[5]. Yes, that was it. First she could weaken the supports, then drag the body there, and when she was ready, she could tie[6] the rope to a support and from a safe distance pull on it until it collapsed.

She went to the supports, leaving the body there, and began to examine them.

She had to be very careful. She had to weaken the support, but not too much.

She took the hammer from her pocket and began to destroy a little of the stone at the top of one of the supports, while constantly listening to the stone.

For ten minutes she worked, slowly and carefully, and then she moved to the other support. She thought this one already

1   **secure –** *fest*
2   **to collapse –** *einstürzen*
3   **vertical –** *senkrecht*
4   **to weaken –** *schwächen*
5   **coil of rope –** *Seilrolle*
6   **to tie –** *festbinden*

looked weaker and after just two minutes she heard the stones about her move. She froze.

Above her she could imagine the ancient pyramid and the hundreds of thousands of blocks of stone. Suddenly, she felt like she should leave the tunnels and Belize, return to Oxford and never enter this horrible place again.

But no, she could not. She had to finish this now.

She ran back to the rope and picked up one end, leaving the other by the body.

For a second, in the shadows, she thought she saw Mounier's eye move. She stopped and stared, but no, it was just a trick of the light.

He was dead. It was an accident, but he was dead.

She walked back to the support and listened.

Silence.

But that did not mean she was safe. She began to tie the rope to the support and had only just finished when she heard it.

At first she thought that it was the stone moving above her, and she believed she was in danger. But then she realised[1] that it was not the stone at all.

It was a weak cry of help from Mounier.

He was alive.

For a second she did not believe it, but then she saw his hands move, and his cry for help was repeated. She felt dizzy[2], and she had no idea what to do.

He was alive, she could still tell the embassy everything. She could tell them that he had attacked her and that it had been an accident and that she had only been trying to defend[3] herself.

Yes, that is what she would do.

But then she saw his hands moving; they were reaching out, searching for something to help him sit.

---

1   **to realise –** *sich klar werden*
2   **dizzy –** *schwindlig*
3   **to defend oneself –** *sich verteidigen*

And then his hand found the rope.

"No! Don't…" she shouted.

But it was too late. The sound of moving stone filled her ears, and dust[1] filled her mouth and eyes. Then everything went black.

Mounier never remembered how he had got so far into the tunnel or exactly what had happened to his assistant. But he knew what to say to the police and the reporters – and to her parents.

And no one could disagree.

Because it had been, obviously, exactly how he described it. An accident.

---

1   **dust –** *Staub*

→ **Belize** ist das einzige Land Zentralamerikas, in dem Englisch die offizielle Amtssprache ist. Heutzutage ist bekannt, dass Belize mitten im Herzen des Gebietes liegt, das die Maya ehemals bewohnt haben. In Belize sind über 900 archäologische Fundstätten zu finden, wo einige der ältesten archäologischen Funde ausgegraben wurden, wie z.B. die Ruine „Cuello" in der Nähe von Orange Walk Town. Viele dieser beeindruckenden Fundstätten befinden sich in sehr abgelegenen Dschungelgegenden. Andere, wie Altun Ha und Xunantunich, liegen sehr nahe an Hauptverkehrsstraßen.

2. COLD HEART

"They say the weather is going to change." John said, looking out of the window of the car as it moved slowly along the quiet road.

Next to him his wife, Jill, continued to drive in silence, and he knew she was still not happy.

For a while he said nothing and enjoyed looking at the snow-covered Lancashire countryside. They had left Manchester half an hour ago and the grey of the city had slowly changed to white.

"It's nearly March. They say this snow should be gone in a few days."

That horrible silence again.

"Jill?"

She turned to look at him for a second, and he thought that his wife could sometimes look extremely terrifying[1].

"Jill, I only said that maybe he's gone because she's always…"

"Always what?" Jill snapped[2], and John knew this was a dangerous conversation.

"You know. Hard. She can be very hard."

Jill shook her head. "She's my best friend, John."

"Well, he's my best mate[3]," John said defensively[4], "and the things he used to say about her…"

"What?"

"Well, she never let him go to the pub. She didn't like him playing football with us on Sunday mornings."

1   **terrifying** – *furchterregend*
2   **to snap** – *aufschnappen*
3   **mate** – *Kumpel*
4   **defensively** – *verteidigend*

"And you think that is a good reason to leave your wife and two children, do you?"

A very dangerous conversation.

They drove in silence for the next five miles until they reached Rawtenstall, a quiet Lancashire town of grey terraced houses[1] and forgotten cotton mills[2].

Jill parked the car and then turned to her husband.

"I'm going to ask you one more time. Do you know where he is?"

John shook his head. "I've told you a hundred times. No."

Jill looked at him carefully. "And he hasn't phoned you? Sent you any texts[3]?"

"No, I promise."

Jill was dangerously silent for another moment. "And tell me the truth, is there another woman?"

The truth. What could he say to that? It was true that he had not seen Phil, that he had not received any calls from him. However, he could not tell her the truth about Phil in regards to[4] other women.

How could he? What could he say?

That he was cheating[5] on his wife? That he had at least three or four women that he was constantly texting[6] or calling from his secret mobile[7]?

No. Obviously he could not say that.

"I don't know. He's never said anything to me about another woman."

For another moment Jill said nothing, but then she shook her head. "Okay, but if he calls or texts you, I want to know."

COLD HEART

---

1   **terraced house –** *Reihenhaus*
2   **cotton mill –** *Baumwollspinnerei*
3   **text (message) –** *SMS*
4   **in regards to –** *bezüglich*
5   **to cheat on sb. –** *jdn. betrügen*
6   **to text –** *simsen*
7   **mobile (phone) –** *Handy*

"Yes, dear," John said, and they got out of the car.

Was Phil with one of his other women?

At first John had thought that he was, but after two weeks he had begun to worry. He had tried to call Phil's secret mobile, the one that Sally did not know about, but there was no reply. And his office knew nothing either: he had not been to work once, and he had not emailed or called them.

"Do you think maybe he's had an accident?" John asked as they walked through the snow towards the house.

"I hope he has because no other reason is good enough. Poor Sally. And those beautiful kids of theirs. If he hasn't had an accident, I will kill him if I ever see him again."

John shivered[1], but he was not sure if it was because of the cold or because of the tone of his wife's voice.

They reached the door of the house.

"Do we have to stay for long?"

Jill gave him a hard look and pressed the doorbell[2].

"I hope she's okay, the poor…"

Then the door opened, and Sally was there. John had always found Sally extremely beautiful, with her warm smile, her friendly eyes and those eyebrows which accompanied every word she said. At least normally.

However, she did not look like this today.

No, today Sally looked completely different. Her hair was untidy[3] and unwashed. Her eyes were dull[4] and tired and had large purple circles under them. And her face looked like it could not smile and that it never had smiled.

"Sally," said Jill. "Oh, Sally, how are you?"

For a moment Sally did not seem to hear and continued to look at them with a strange expression on her face.

---

1   **to shiver –** *erschaudern*
2   **doorbell –** *Türklingel*
3   **untidy –** *zerstrubbelt*
4   **dull –** *stumpf*

"Oh, Jill, John. You're here."

"Yes, we said we were coming today. Don't you remember?"

Sally nodded. "Of course, of course. Come in," she said and walked back into the house.

For a moment they hesitated[1]. "Jesus, she looks…" John began.

"Shh, come on."

They had been to Sally and Phil's place hundreds of times, but the house had never looked like this. Normally the small but attractive terraced house was perfectly organised and immaculately[2] clean. However, today there were children's toys lying on every inch of the floor, baskets of dirty clothes blocking the hallway and a smell of rubbish and old food from the kitchen.

They found Sally in the lounge[3] sitting on the sofa and watched as she poured herself a glass of wine.

"Drink?" she said, but John and Jill both shook their heads.

"Oh, Sally, you poor thing[4]. Do you still know nothing?"

Sally looked confused for a moment, and then unexpectedly she laughed. "No, Jill, I know everything. Everything."

"What? You know where Phil is?"

She laughed again. "Oh yes. But I know a lot more than that. I know about the other women. I found his phone. I read all his dirty messages."

"Other women?" Jill said, and she gave John a quick, terrifying look.

"Lots. I don't know how many."

"Oh my God. How could he? The monster. I always thought he had a cold heart, but I never thought…"

"What?" Sally said, a strange expression growing on her face. "What did you say?"

---

1   **to hesitate** – *zögern*
2   **immaculately** – *makellos*
3   **lounge** – *Salon*
4   **poor thing** – *armes Ding*

COLD HEART

"I… just that Phil has a cold heart."

And for a moment it seemed like Sally might cry, but she began to laugh instead and she laughed so hard that her hand shook and the wine splashed from the glass onto the coffee table.

Jill looked at John in confusion[1], but he shook his head.

"What, Sally? What is it?" Jill asked, and she went to sit next to her friend and took the glass of wine from her.

"A cold heart! Ha, oh yes, oh yes! That's good, that's very good!" Sally said, and she laughed for another minute before she finally stopped.

"But do you know where he is now?" Jill asked.

"Oh, yes, of course."

"You do? Where?"

"He's here."

"Here?" John asked, surprised.

"Won't you have a drink?" Sally said to Jill.

"But where is he?" John asked again.

"Oh, he's outside in the garden, with the kids."

"But the other women?" Jill asked.

"Oh, there won't be any more of them," Sally said, and she smiled in a way that made John feel cold.

"I think I'll go say hello," he said, but the two women ignored him.

He walked to the kitchen, which was dirty, the bin full and rubbish in bags next to it, and he looked out of the window. The garden was white, the snow half a metre high, and he could see the kids, little Sammy and Sarah, playing in the snow.

But he could not see Phil.

He went to the door and opened it. "Hey, kids," he shouted, and they waved at him and smiled.

"Where's your dad then?" But their faces were blank[2], and they shook their heads.

---

1 **confusion –** *Verwirrung*
2 **blank –** *ausdruckslos*

"He must be upstairs, hey?" he said, and he shut the door, and they began to play again. Making snowballs and throwing them at the large snowman in the middle of the garden.

"I made a mistake," Sally said behind him, and John jumped with fright[1]. He turned round and looked at her.

"Where's Phil?"

"I was confused," Sally said, her voice strange. "I have not been sleeping very well. Phil's not here. I don't know where he is."

John nodded. "I see."

And for the next two hours Jill helped to tidy the house and talked to Sally and told her that Phil was a monster. Then it was time to go.

"Goodbye then," Jill said. "I'll come back in a few days, but if you need anything, you call me, okay?"

Sally nodded and showed them to the door[2], and John felt like he should say something, but he did not know what.

"Oh well, everything will be okay, hey? And at least the weather is improving. All this snow should be gone in a few days."

"What?" Sally said, and she grabbed his arm, "What did you say?"

And her fingers pressed into his skin so hard that he almost shouted for her to stop.

"The weather… is improving," he said.

"The snow… you said… the snow…."

And then something horrible occurred to John. No, it could not possibly be true.

"Sally? Phil… you didn't?"

Sally smiled. Then she began to laugh again, and in between the laughter she repeated two words.

Two words.

John took his phone from his pocket and pushed past Sally. He went into the kitchen and opened the back door.

COLD HEART

---

1 **fright** – *Erschrecken*
2 **to show sb. to the door** – *jdn. zur Tür bringen*

"What are you doing, John?" Jill shouted.

Two words.

He pressed "call" on the number of Phil's secret phone and walked out into the snow and stood before the snowman.

It was true: from somewhere deep inside the snow, he heard the sound of a ringing phone.

Behind him he heard Sally laughing and Jill shouting.

But he could only think about those two words.

"Cold heart."

Die Stadt Rawtenstall liegt in der Grafschaft **Lancashire** im Nordwesten Englands, der als die Wiege der industriellen Revolution gilt. Die Gegend ist berühmt für ihre Rolle in der Geschichte der Industrie im ausgehenden 18. Jahrhundert und die daraus resultierende Architektur. Zunächst herrschte die Baumwollindustrie vor, die auch eine sehr rasante Entwicklung erfuhr. Diese Entwicklung bescherte der Region ein hochentwickeltes Transportsystem zu Land und Wasser. Beispielhaft dafür ist die weltweit erste Städteverbindung mit der Eisenbahn zwischen Manchester und Liverpool.

3. THE LOCKED ROOM

Victoria looked out of the glass elevator[1] and watched the city of Houston in front of her.

The city was a sea of lights and the lift continued to rise[2] until she was higher than all of the other skyscrapers[3].

She turned to the handsome Japanese man who stood silently next to her and shook her head[4]. "I still don't understand what I'm doing here," she said as they continued to rise.

Mr Ichiro nodded. "I know, and I'm sorry to wake you at this time of the night, but when you agreed to write for the Teikoku Company, you signed a contract... And in this contract you agreed to be available[5] for Mr Kenta at any time."

"You always say that, but I don't remember any agreement[6]. And what type of assistance can he need from me? I'm a writer, a novelist[7]."

Ichiro nodded. "I know. You met Mr Kenta when you started to work at the company; he was very pleased to meet you."

"He's a nice man, and he seems to like my writing, but I still don't understand why he needs to see me."

"Ah, no, he doesn't. You don't understand. You can't see Mr Kenta, but he wants you to help me with a problem. He was always very impressed with your stories and your beautifully complex plots[8]."

1	**elevator** – *(AE) Aufzug*
2	**to rise** – *hinaufsteigen*
3	**skyscraper** – *Wolkenkratzer*
4	**to shake one's head** – *den Kopf schütteln*
5	**available** – *verfügbar*
6	**agreement** – *Vereinbarung*
7	**novelist** – *Schriftsteller(in)*
8	**plot** – *Handlung*

Victoria looked at Ichiro: the man's English was almost perfect, but for a moment she thought he had made a mistake. "You said, he *was* always impressed."

And then she saw the emotion that Ichiro was trying to hide[1]. "Yes, Mr Kenta is dead. He was killed this evening. Murdered."

It took Victoria a moment to understand. "He's dead? But you said that he wanted me to help you."

"That's correct. Mr Kenta left a very detailed will[2]. In his will he stated that if he died in mysterious circumstances[3], he wanted you to assist me in identifying his killer."

"What? That's crazy. You don't need me, you need the police."

"The police are here, but the Teikoku Company is very powerful, and the Houston police have agreed to you seeing the murder scene[4]." The lift stopped, and Ichiro looked at her.

The metal doors opened and outside two paramedics[5] and a Houston cop were waiting. Between them a gurney[6], which was carrying a black body bag[7].

Mr Ichiro bowed[8] and looked at the bag with an expression of sadness. "Please wait in the car park for me. I wish to travel to the hospital with the body."

The cop nodded, and Victoria stepped from the lift so they could enter.

Ichiro passed her a pair of latex gloves. "I know you are familiar with crime scenes because of your research, but remember to touch nothing without these."

---

1   **to hide** – *verbergen*
2   **will** – *Testament*
3   **in mysterious circumstances** – *unter mysteriösen Umständen*
4   **murder scene** – *Tatort*
5   **paramedic** – *Sanitäter(in)*
6   **gurney** – *(AE) Rollbahre*
7   **body bag** – *Leichensack*
8   **to bow** – *sich verbeugen*

Victoria watched the elevator door close. "Okay, but if this is real, if you want my help, shouldn't I[1] see the body?"

"You can, if you wish, but I examined it," Ichiro said, "and I can tell you he was killed by a knife or dagger[2] to his heart. It looks professional. He died… without pain."

Victoria nodded.

"That, however, is not the problem. The problem is how the murderer escaped. Follow me."

They walked along a luxurious corridor[3] to a large golden door where two policemen and two private security guards were waiting.

Ichiro nodded and a security guard opened the door.

The room inside was more spectacular than any other room Victoria had ever seen. It was like a Japanese palace in the sky, with elaborate[4] decorations, modern and classical art, expensive furniture and every type of electronic device possible.

"Yes, when you met Mr Kenta, you saw his private offices. This is his personal apartment within the Teikoku Company. It was his place to connect to his origins in Japan. Mr Kenta needed this."

There were blood stains on the white carpets and the black leather sofas. "Did he die here?"

"Yes."

"Did you find him?"

"I did. I'm Mr Kenta's head of security," he said, and Victoria could hear the shame[5] in his voice.

"I saw cameras in the corridor."

THE LOCKED ROOM

1   **shouldn't I...** – *sollte ich nicht...*
2   **dagger** – *Dolch*
3   **corridor** – *Flur*
4   **elaborate** – *kunstvoll*
5   **shame** – *Schamgefühl*

"Yes, but there are none[1] in here. He was a private man[2]. And I assured him that he was safe[3] here… but I was wrong."

"Why did you think he was safe?"

"Because there is only one access point[4] to this room: the corridor. The only other way is to climb[5] the glass walls of the building and enter one of the windows here. That climb is almost impossible, and the windows can only be opened from inside. But more than this, the apartment is protected by one of the best security systems in the world, imported from Japan, and nobody but[6] Mr Kenta and I knew the activation words. Watch." Ichiro said something in Japanese.

Suddenly there was movement in every part of the room, and metal screens fell from the roof on the inside and outside of the windows. The golden door closed instantly[7], and Victoria heard an electronic lock connect.

"As soon as that command is given[8] the police are informed, I am informed, my team is informed."

"Impressive, but obviously Mr Kenta didn't have enough time to give the command."

Ichiro shook his head. "You don't understand. When I arrived the room was locked."

Victoria thought for a second and then she suddenly understood. "Then the killer didn't escape. If Kenta died instantly, he probably gave the command a second before his death."

"Exactly," said Ichiro, and Victoria noticed for the first time that his hand was always near to the gun under his jacket.

"You think he's still in this room?"

1	**none –** *keine*
2	**private man –** *zurückhaltender Mann*
3	**safe –** *in Sicherheit*
4	**access point –** *Zugangspunkt*
5	**to climb –** *klettern*
6	**nobody but –** *niemand außer*
7	**instantly –** *augenblicklich*
8	**As soon as that command is given… –** *Sobald dieser Befehl erteilt wird…*

"It's impossible. We've searched[1] every place a man could hide. The police and my team tell me that there is nobody here."

"What do you think?"

"I think this system is the best. When Mr Kenta gave the command, the room was locked. How could the killer escape?"

Victoria nodded. It was, indeed, like the plot of one of her novels[2]: an impossible murder.

She walked around the room slowly and for some time considered the possibilities. They were few.

Could the killer still be here?

"Did your men check the outside of the building? Perhaps there was a delay in the system."

"They are checking now. A helicopter searched the glass walls but saw nobody. The men are searching some of the lower levels."

Victoria was silent. She watched Ichiro. "There is another possibility," she began.

"Yes, there is."

"You're the only other person who can control the security system. You were the first to find the body."

Ichiro looked at her. "Mr Kenta was correct: you are good. But I can assure you that I was in the security room. I have witnesses[3] and there is video evidence. But more than this, I can tell you that Mr Kenta was like a father to me. He brought me from Japan to Houston. I will find his killer and I will find the people who paid the killer, for[4] I believe this was an assassination[5] by a rival American company. They were jealous of our success. I am guilty only of my inability[6] to protect him."

Victoria said nothing, but she believed the man.

THE LOCKED ROOM

---

1 **to search** – *durchsuchen*
2 **novel** – *Roman*
3 **witness** – *Augenzeuge*
4 **for** – *denn*
5 **assassination** – *Ermordung*
6 **inability** – *Unfähigkeit*

She was about to[1] speak, when Ichiro's radio broke the silence. For a moment the head of security listened and Victoria saw a dark expression on his face.

"What? What is it?" she asked.

"They have found a body. Thirteen floors below on the roof of the second tower. I think I woke you for no reason, but thank you."

Victoria nodded, but she did not move.

"What is it?" asked Ichiro, seeing her doubt.

"It makes no sense. How could the killer escape? Mr Kenta gave the command the second before his death, and the room locked. There was no time for the killer to go back to the window."

Ichiro nodded. "Perhaps there was a fault in the system[2]?"

"And now there is no fault? I don't think so[3]." And she moved to the window again and looked at the city of Houston and the sea of lights and watched an ambulance racing through the streets.

And suddenly she understood: "Ichiro, the body: can they identify it?"

"No: the fall was too high. It's impossible to recognise."

"And after the murder was there always someone here in the room?"

"No, but there were always guards at the door, and the helicopter was also there."

"No one climbed down, Ichiro: they fell. I'm sorry, but the body they have found is Mr Kenta."

"What?"

"I think that for a few moments after the paramedics arrived, after they placed Mr Kenta's body in the bag, the room was empty, but the killer was still here."

"We searched the room."

---

1 **to be about to do sth.** – *im Begriff sein, etw. zu tun*
2 **fault in the system** – *Systemfehler*
3 **I don't think so.** – *Ich glaube nicht.*

"Yes, but before or after the paramedics arrived?"

"Before and after."

"But there are many places to hide, and I think that when you first looked, you didn't find him, but he was here. Then, later, after the paramedics arrived, you looked in every possible place, but he was gone."

"How? He didn't walk out the door."

"No, he didn't: he was pushed... on a gurney."

And for a second Ichiro did not understand, but then his expression changed, and he ran through the golden door to the lift, his hand on his gun.

But Victoria knew that it was too late: he would find[1] only two dead paramedics, a dead cop and an empty body bag.

THE LOCKED ROOM

---

1   **he would find...** – *er würde finden...*

Houston wurde 1836 von zwei Unternehmern aus New York gegründet. Die Stadt hatte im Jahr 1900 noch weniger als 50.000 Einwohner. Doch kurz danach wurde der Hafen eröffnet und die Stadt begann unaufhaltsam zu wachsen. Heute ist sie mit 2,2 Millionen Einwohnern die viertgrößte Stadt in den USA und der Hafen gilt als der wichtigste Hafen Amerikas. Wegen des Mission Control Centers, das sich hier befindet, trägt Houston den Spitznamen Space City. Von hier aus hat die NASA viele Fahrten ins All begleitet, unter anderem den berühmten Apollo 11 Flug. Übrigens lautete die berühmte Meldung der Astronauten damals nicht „Houston, we have a problem", wie häufig wiedergegeben wird, sondern Jack Swigert meldete an die Bodenstation: „Okay, Houston, we've had a problem here."

4. THE HONEY TRAP

Charles loved New York in the summer time. It was an absolute paradise for a man of his profession, and this evening he was feeling extremely happy about his recent work.

He sat back[1] in his chair at the small coffee shop table and watched the hundreds of people stroll[2] past him. Occasionally, he saw something that made him laugh, things that maybe you or I would not find funny, such as a visible[3] wallet in the back pocket of a man's jeans, or an open bag on the shoulder of a woman.

To you or me these things would not be amusing[4]: in fact[5], we would not even notice them. To Charles, however, they were a constant source of pleasure.

Charles was a perfectly normal man. There was absolutely nothing unusual about his appearance. He was of average height and weight, with ordinary brown hair and an unremarkable[6] face.

He was the type of man that nobody ever remembered.

And this is what made Charles very good at his job.

He saw the waitress and politely signaled[7] to her. "The bill, please."

"Oh my gosh![8] Are you English? What an awesome[9] accent you have."

1	**to sit back** – *sich zurücklehnen*
2	**to stroll** – *schlendern*
3	**visible** – *sichtbar*
4	**amusing** – *amüsierend*
5	**in fact** – *eigentlich*
6	**unremarkable** – *unscheinbar*
7	**to signal to sb.** – *jdm. ein Zeichen geben*
8	**Oh my gosh!** – *Oh mein Gott!*
9	**awesome** – *(AE) super*

She placed the bill for his drink on the table.

Charles smiled and put down five dollars. "Thank you very much. Please, keep the change."

"Thank you!" she smiled and began to walk away.

"Oh, excuse me? I don't suppose you can change a twenty[1]? I need some dollar bills[2] for the subway[3]."

"Sure![4] Here you go, ten ones and a ten."

"Excellent," Charles said, taking the notes. "Oh, look, actually I have some change[5] here. Now I think I have too much. Could I change the ones back for a ten?"

"Of course," said the waitress with another smile. "Here's your ten."

He took it and seemed to put it in his wallet. "And here are your dollars," he said with an apologetic smile. "Is that right?"

"I'm sure it is… oh no, that's only nine dollars," she said and put the dollars on the table for him to see.

"Oh dear, this American money, it all looks the same to me. Well, because I have change I can take my twenty back. There's nine there, so I can give you a one and a ten, right?"

The waitress smiled again but looked a little confused now. "Oh, of course, and here's your twenty."

"Excellent. Thank you," he said, and the waitress watched him walk away.

Charles shook his head and looked at the ten dollars that he had just made, but he did not feel any sympathy for[6] the poor waitress. His motto was that if a person could be conned[7], they should be conned.

---

1   **I don't suppose you can change a twenty?** – *Könnten Sie einen Zwanziger wechseln?*
2   **bill** – *(AE) Geldschein*
3   **subway** – *(AE) U-Bahn*
4   **Sure!** – *Klar!*
5   **change** – *Kleingeld*
6   **to feel sympathy for sb.** – *mit jdm. Mitleid haben*
7   **to con sb.** – *jdn. betrügen*

A little further along the road, he saw another cafe, and outside two women were sitting and talking. One of their purses[1] was on their table.

He smiled and took his map of New York from his pocket.

"G'day![2] I don't suppose you can help me?" he said in a strong Australian accent.

The two women looked at him with interest. "Sure, what's the problem?"

"I'm looking for this street," he said and put the map over the table, so they could see.

"Oh, that's easy, just turn left here."

"Really? Well, that's great ladies, thanks a lot."

And they watched him go with smiles on their faces too, and neither noticed that the purse was no longer on the table.

Charles was happy as he entered the park, but these small tricks were only for his amusement[3]. Shortly[4] he would meet his assistant, and the real work could start.

He approached the bench where they had arranged to meet, but she was not there. He looked at his watch; there were still a few minutes left.

Nearby[5] a violinist was playing music and seven or eight people had stopped to listen. One man had his jacket over his shoulder and Charles could see his wallet.

Not easy, he thought, but not impossible.

The violinist's song finished, and Charles stepped forward to place some money in the case at the musician's feet. Nobody seemed to notice that[6] instead of giving a dollar he took three.

Then he turned, took his newspaper from under his arm and started to open it. Unfortunately, it seemed that he had not

---

1   **purse** - *Geldbeutel*
2   **G'day!** - *(AUS) Guten Tag!*
3   **for his amusement** - *zu seinem Vergnügen*
4   **shortly** - *in Kürze*
5   **nearby** - *in der Nähe*
6   **Nobody seemed to notice that...** - *Niemand schien zu bemerken, dass...*

seen the man with the jacket over his shoulder. He apologised for accidentally bumping into[1] him. He then continued to walk with the man's wallet safely hidden in his newspaper.

He sat on the bench and hid his new items in the many pockets in his brown suit. And then he saw her.

His new assistant, Honey.

"Hey, Charles," she said.

"Good evening, Honey. You're late."

"Relax, he won't be here for another five minutes."

"Yes, but we need to make sure you understand the plan."
"Of course I do: it's exactly the same as with the other guys," she said in her strong New York accent.

Charles nodded. She was right. The plan was the same, but she did not seem to realise that this time it was for real. The other two guys they had trapped[2] were just for practice. Sure, they had made a little money, but tonight they could make a lot.

"And are you sure he's going to kiss you out here? I mean, he needs to be careful."

"Oh, I'm sure. I told him I don't want to meet him in some horrible hotel room. That if he likes me he can meet me outside. So I guess he might do something with his hair or wear a hat, you know, like a disguise[3]."

"True. But if he does, you have to make sure that when you kiss him I can see his face."

"No problem."

"Are you sure you saw his account properly? Are you sure he can withdraw five grand[4]?"

"I watched him do it the other day. He has a five grand limit. I mean, the guy is rich, really rich."

---

1   **to bump into sb.** – *mit jdm. zusammenstoßen*
2   **to trap sb.** – *jdn. in die Falle locken*
3   **disguise** – *Tarnung*
4   **grand** – *(ugs.) Riese, Tausender*

"Okay, so after we trap him, I take him to the ATM[1] and then we meet back here. Remember: if anything goes wrong, you don't know me."

"Sure, I don't know you."

"I'm serious, Honey. If the police find out that we're working together, we're in trouble."

"Okay."

Charles nodded, looked at her golden dress and beautiful hair and almost felt sorry for the guy.

Then he moved into the trees near the bench and took the camera from around his neck.

For a few minutes he watched his assistant sitting alone on the bench. Then he noticed a well-dressed good-looking man walking in her direction. The man was wearing sunglasses and kept his face down to the ground. He sat down next to Honey and they began to talk. Then, after a while, the man took her hand and moved closer to her. Charles saw Honey remove his sunglasses.

Yes, it was him, Mr Harris, the CEO[2] of Harris Enterprises.

Honey smiled and put her arm around him. For a second Harris did nothing, but he could not resist her charms[3] for long, and soon he kissed her.

Charles took the photo, and then came out from his hiding position.

"What the hell[4]? What are you doing?" Harris shouted.

"Sorry Mr Harris, but she paid me to," he said in a perfect Scottish accent.

Harris looked at Honey. "Honey?"

"No, not her, Mrs Harris, your wife."

"What? No!"

---

1   **ATM –** *(AE) Geldautomat*
2   **CEO (Chief Executive Officer) –** *Geschäftsführer(in)*
3   **to resist sb.'s charms –** *dem Charme von jemandem widerstehen*
4   **What the hell? –** *Was zum Teufel?*

"Aye[1], I'm a private detective. She contracted me to follow you and to take photos of… well, this type of activity."

Harris' face went white. "God, no, I'm ruined. She's gonna tell the press. My business, my clients. I'm gonna lose everything."

"You creep. You never told me you were married!" Honey shouted, and she stood up, her face furious, and walked in the direction of the park's exit.

"Sorry, pal[2], but it's my job."

"Look, you said she paid you," said Harris. "How much?"

Charles hesitated.

"Whatever it is, I can give you double."

"Double? Well, Mrs Harris said she would give me three grand for a photo."

"Three grand? Right, then I'll give you six."

"I don't know. Can you get it now?"

Harris hesitated. "Well, I can get you five now."

"You said six."

Harris nodded. "Okay, I have about a grand in my wallet, but I need to go to the ATM for the other five."

"Yeah, well I think I'll come with you," Charles said, trying not to smile.

But when they got to the ATM, Harris began to search his wallet.

"Jesus!" he shouted. "My card, I don't have my card!"

"What?"

"Look, take the grand for now, and let me send you the rest."

Charles agreed. He had to, but he was sure he would never see the money. All Harris had to do was say something to his wife, and he would realise it was all a con.

Alone and unhappy, Charles walked back to the park to find Honey.

A perfect evening ruined because the idiot had lost his card. Lost his card?

He remembered the way Honey had put her arm around him. He remembered how Honey had said she had seen his account.

Did she know his PIN[1] too?

A suspicion[2] began to form in Charles' mind.

In that moment he saw Honey, a hundred metres in front of him, near to the bench.

And he saw the cop that was holding her by the arm.

Then Honey saw him, and Charles saw her point in his direction, and the cop looked too.

And that is when Charles decided to run.

"Is that him, miss? Why's he running?" the cop asked Honey.

"Yeah, that's the man who helped me when I fell over. Thank you, my leg feels better now," she said, in a perfect English accent. "But I don't know why he's running: he seemed like such a nice man," she added.

She thought about the five thousand dollars she had just withdrawn from the ATM and she smiled. But she almost felt sorry to lose such a good assistant as Charles.

---

1   **PIN -** *Geheimzahl*
2   **suspicion -** *Verdacht*

→ Der **Central Park**, auch grüne Lunge New Yorks genannt, fehlt in keinem Reiseführer über die Stadt. Es lohnt sich, ihn von einem der Wolkenkratzer aus der unmittelbaren Umgebung einmal von oben zu betrachten, um die Größe seiner Anlage zu begreifen. Diese macht mit über 349 Hektaren etwa 4 Prozent der Bodenfläche Manhattans aus. Die Bauarbeiten für den Park begannen 1858 und ließen auf dem ehemaligen Sumpfgelände einen See, ein ganzes Netz an Straßen und Pfaden, einen Zoo, eine Burg und vieles mehr entstehen. Die Planer des Parks galten 1859-60 als größter Arbeitgeber der Stadt und konnten es sich erlauben, die Bauarbeiter unter unwürdigen Bedingungen arbeiten zu lassen, da „problematische" Arbeitskräfte leicht ersetzt werden konnten.

5. THE MURDER MYSTERY

Detective Harp lifted an old newspaper above his head and ran from his car to the entrance of Heartfelt Manor[1]. The night was dark and wet, the storm was still over the mountains of the Lake District, and by the time he had reached the door his dark hair and beard were dripping[2] with rain water.

In the hallway Sergeant Sloane was waiting for him, the officer's face as white as a ghost.

"Where is everyone, Sloane?"

"It's just me here, sir. There was an accident on the old road, and no other officers can get here at the moment. But I'm glad you're here, sir: this is a real mess."

Harp nodded and looked around. He had lived near to Heartfelt Manor for twenty years, but he had never been inside. It was even more luxurious than he had imagined, with expensive portraits and the heads of stags[3] and other animals on the walls, and a blood-red carpet that covered the large staircase[4].

"So what do you know, Sloane?"

"Not much, sir. The body[5] is in the library. There are seven people in the house: Mr and Mrs Grey, their three guests and two employees, the cook and the maid[6]. At approximately half past eight there was a power cut[7], probably because of the storm,

1	**manor (house)** – *Herrenhaus*
2	**to drip** – *tropfen*
3	**stag** – *Hirsch*
4	**staircase** – *Treppenhaus*
5	**body** – *Leiche*
6	**maid** – *Dienstmädchen*
7	**power cut** – *Stromausfall*

and everyone heard a scream. The maid was the first to find the body. I've asked her and the cook to stay in the kitchen for now, and the others are in the conservatory[1]."

"Show me the body," Harp said, and he followed Sloane to the library.

The room was large and cold, and the fire in the corner looked like it had been extinguished[2] earlier that evening. There were only a few weak electric lights to illuminate[3] the scene and the hundreds of books that lined[4] the walls.

The body was at the table, a strange knife sticking out from his back, and a pool of blood around him on the floor.

"It's like something from that game, isn't it, sir? You know, the library, the conservatory, a dead body. And we have to find out who did it."

Harp shook his head. "This is not a game: this is a real murder," he said, but Harp knew what Sloane meant, and he remembered that he had always hated that game when he was a child.

"Yes, sir. Sorry sir," Sloane said.

"It's alright," Harp said with half a smile. "Maybe the butler did it, hey?"

"No, sir," said Sloane, not noticing the joke, "this is the butler, sir."

Harp looked at the black suit the man was wearing and saw that Sloane was right.

"What do we do, sir?"

Harp looked around the room more carefully. There was a collection of letter openers[5] next to some writing equipment on the desk, and Harp believed this is where the murder weapon had come from. By the extinguished fire there was a half-empty

---

1   **conservatory** – *Wintergarten*
2   **to extinguish** – *auslöschen*
3   **to illuminate** – *beleuchten*
4   **to line** – *säumen*
5   **letter opener** – *Brieföffner*

jug[1] of water next to two unused glasses. He walked to the fire and looked at it carefully. On top of it were the remains[2] of some sort of papers, destroyed by the flames and water so that they were now impossible to read.

"Alibi and motive," he said. "I want to speak to Mr Grey and his guests. I will speak to them all at the same time, and we can see if their stories match[3]."

"And the cook and the maid?"

"No, not until later."

And Harp followed Sloane back into the hallway.

"Is it true then?" said a woman's voice, and they turned to see a middle-aged[4] woman in a white uniform, "Is he dead? Is Edmund really dead?"

"I'm sorry, but yes."

The woman nodded, and Harp could see tears in her eyes.

"He was not exactly a good man, you know, but he was okay with me. Here," and the cook passed Harp a large file of papers. "Edmund told me that if anything ever happened to him I must give this to the police."

"What is it?"

"I don't know. He just said it was important."

Harp nodded but did not open the file: he had no time for this now as he needed to speak to the guests.

"Sloane, take her back to the kitchen and take statements from her and the maid. Is this the conservatory?" he asked, looking at two large glass doors.

Sloane nodded, and Harp pushed open the doors.

Inside the conservatory five faces turned to look at him, and Harp had the very clear sensation[5] that one of these people was his murderer.

---

1   **jug –** *Krug*
2   **remain –** *Rest*
3   **to match –** *übereinstimmen*
4   **middle-aged –** *mittleren Alters*
5   **sensation –** *Eindruck*

"My name is Detective Harp. I need to speak to you about what happened this evening."

A tall man with white hair stepped forwards. "I'm Mr Grey; this is my wife Jennifer," he said, looking at a much younger and very attractive blonde. "These are our guests, Alexander Pine, Miss Olivia Blake and her brother, Reverend[1] Blake."

"I see. And the deceased[2]?"

"Our butler, Edmund. A good man. Very capable[3]. He has been with us for nearly ten years now."

"And there was no one else in the house this evening?"

"No."

"I see. Then I must ask you all to inform me of exactly where you were when you heard the scream."

"What? You don't think any of us are involved, do you?" asked Olivia, a plain[4] young woman with brown hair and glasses.

"It's procedure[5]."

"Well, I can tell you where I was," said the reverend. "In the dining room finishing my brandy. The lights went out, and then there was a scream."

"I see."

"And I was in my bedroom changing my dress," Mrs Grey said. "I had spilled some wine on it during dinner."

"Oh yes, I remember you saying that. I was actually in here. I was looking for the chess board[6] so that Alexander and I could play," said Mr Grey, and he smiled at the younger man.

"Yes, and I was in the study[7]. I wanted to finish a poem I had been thinking about. I'm a poet, you see?" Alexander said.

---

1   **reverend – *Pastor***
2   **deceased – *Verstorbene(r)***
3   **capable – *tüchtig***
4   **plain – *unscheinbar***
5   **procedure – *Standardprozedur***
6   **chess board – *Schachbrett***
7   **study – *Arbeitszimmer***

"And Miss Blake?"

"Well, I think, yes, I was in the hall. I was about to enter the conservatory when the lights went out, and I heard the scream."

Harp shook his head. "So you were all in different parts of the house. And none of you can confirm the location[1] of anyone else."

"Do we have to? Don't you believe us?" Mrs Grey asked.

Harp was about to respond when Sloane opened the door, and Harp went to speak to him. "The station just called on the radio, sir. They need me to help with the accident on the old road. I should be back here in an hour."

"That's fine. Everything is under control here," he said, and after a moment he heard Sloane leave the manor house and the sound of his police car driving out into the storm.

He was about to continue questioning the guests when he remembered the file that the cook had given him, and he put it down on a table and opened it.

The first thing he saw was a picture of two men in bed together. One of the men was tall with white hair, and although[2] his face was hidden[3], he knew it was the owner of Heartfelt. The other was the young writer Alexander Pine.

He looked up quickly, but Mr Grey and his guests were talking quietly and not looking in his direction. He turned the page and saw a picture of an attractive blonde entering a pharmacy, and behind it were copies of prescriptions for a multitude[4] of strange drugs[5].

He turned the page again and saw a picture of Miss Blake in the street, and some distance in front of her was the same young man who had been in the picture with Mr Grey, Alexander Pine. In fact, there were more than ten pictures of Miss Blake,

---

1 **location** − *Stelle*
2 **although** − *obgleich*
3 **hidden** − *versteckt*
4 **multitude** − *Vielzahl*
5 **drug** − *Medikament*

and in all of them she seemed to be following the young writer, with a strange expression of devotion[1] on her face.

Finally, there was a newspaper article about a hit-and-run accident[2], and behind the article there was a picture of Reverend Blake standing next to a car with two broken lights and something that was maybe red paint or maybe blood on the number plate[3].

Alibi and motive.

An affair.

A woman with a drug problem.

A stalker.

And a respectable man possibly guilty[4] of a hit and run.

Good God, there was evidence in here to suspect that each person in the room had a motive to kill the butler.

He remembered the scene of the murder. The extinguished fire, the destroyed papers.

Had the butler met with one of these people in the library? Was he blackmailing[5] one of them? Had that person tried to burn the papers? Had the butler tried to extinguish the fire? Then, in the darkness of the power cut, had that same person taken one of the letter openers and killed him?

Harp was sure that his suspicions were right.

But who was it?

He looked up, suddenly aware that the room was silent, and saw that the five suspects were watching him.

"What is that?" asked the reverend, his voice dangerously quiet.

"I think you know what this is," Harp said. "In fact, I think maybe you all know what this is."

---

1   **devotion –** *Ergebenheit*
2   **hit-and-run accident –** *Unfall mit Fahrerflucht*
3   **number plate –** *Nummernschild*
4   **guilty –** *schuldig*
5   **to blackmail sb. –** *jdn. erpressen*

There was the sound of thunder outside, and the lights flickered[1] for a moment.

"Why don't you give that to me?" Mr Grey said, and he began to walk forwards.

"This is evidence. This means each one of you had a motive to kill the butler."

"Yes," said Miss Blake, who was also now approaching Harp. "But if you think about it, doesn't that also mean that we have a motive to kill you?" And now Alexander Pine and Mrs Grey were also edging forward[2].

Detective Harp suddenly understood. He could see it now, in their eyes, in all of their eyes.

He was about to tell them to stop, to keep away from him, but there was the sound of thunder again, and the lights flickered, and then there was complete darkness.

And then there was another scream in Heartfelt Manor.

---

1   **to flicker –** *flimmern*
2   **to edge forward –** *sich langsam vorwärtsbewegen*

The **Lake District** ist ein Ort natürlicher Schönheit und liegt in der Grafschaft Cumbria, im Nordwesten Englands. Der Bezirk ist einer der 14 Nationalparks des Vereinigten Königreichs und kann nicht nur mit dem höchsten Berg Englands aufwarten, dem Scafell Pike, sondern auch mit dem tiefsten See (Wastwater) und dem längsten See (Windermere). Die Briten assoziieren diese Gegend mit deren Dichtern und Literaten aus dem frühen 19. Jahrhundert, wie z.B. William Wordsworth. Die Gegend ist aber auch für die Schafszucht bekannt, die neben dem Tourismus die wichtigste Einkommensquelle darstellt.

6. SEE NO EVIL

The summer shower had only just stopped, and the sandstone[1] buildings of Edinburgh were still wet with rain. The evening was warm, however, and Cadha was happy about that.

Next to her, Old Fraser began to move. "Time to be going. The soup kitchen[2] at St. Mary's opens at nine, and there's going to be a queue tonight."

Cadha said nothing. She never did, but she shook her head, and the old man understood. "Ah, going to see the boy? Well, I won't tell you not to, but I will tell you to be careful."

Cadha smiled.

"I know you're canny[3] enough, but the city can be a dangerous place during the festival. Just be careful, and meet me at St Mary's later."

Cadha nodded, stood up and stretched[4]. They had been sitting under the doorway[5] for an hour. Now she wanted to move, to run, to feel the freedom of the city.

She smiled at Old Fraser and then began to walk quickly down the street. It was almost eight o'clock on Tuesday evening, her favourite time of the week.

She looked up at the castle that sat above the city and thought about how far her destination was.

She was late.

1	**sandstone –** *Sandstein*
2	**soup kitchen –** *Armenküche*
3	**canny –** *schlau*
4	**to stretch –** *sich strecken*
5	**doorway –** *Eingang*

The streets were still quiet after the rain, but soon the tourists and businessmen would start to leave their shops, cafes and offices.

So she began to run.

And she ran like a person who knew exactly where to put each foot. Like a person who knew every stone in the city. Every street, every turn.

Because she did. Because the streets were her home, and they were the only home she had.

When she finally reached her destination, she was hot and sweaty[1], but she felt better. She felt more alive.

She jogged across a small park that separated two streets and then climbed onto an old wall.

And she could hear it. She could hear the music.

She smiled and lay back[2].

When she had first found the music, she had known none of the names of the pieces[3], but Fraser had sometimes come to listen too, and the old man had told her about Chopin and Beethoven. Now Cadha listened to them all like an expert.

After twenty minutes she moved.

She jumped from the wall to a tall old tree and turned to the window in the second floor of the house - and she saw him.

She thought he was probably about her age, fourteen or fifteen.

His teacher, an older woman, sat next to him by the piano, and for another half hour they practised[4]. The boy never looked out of the window for the whole time.

Then, at almost nine o'clock, the teacher stood, moved to another part of the room, and the boy began to play. He played the same song that he always played before the end of his lesson, the song that Cadha loved the most[5].

---

1   **sweaty** – *verschwitzt*
2   **to lie back** – *sich zurücklegen*
3   **piece** – *Musikstück*
4   **to practise** – *üben*
5   **the most** – *am meisten*

Beethoven's Moonlight Sonata.

And just before he finished the sonata, he looked up out of the window and smiled.

He always smiled, but Cadha never knew if he could see her hiding there in the trees. Normally she smiled too and waited for him to finish, but this time she moved her lips silently, and formed the two words she had wanted to say to him for a long time.

Thank you.

Then the music finished, and Cadha climbed down from the tree and waited near the wall. After a few moments the door opened, and she saw the boy.

Cadha looked at the sky. It was almost dark, and she knew she should go to meet Fraser if she wanted to eat, but she did not move.

Maybe it was Fraser's warning about the city being more dangerous during the festival, but she decided that she would follow the boy for a few minutes. Just to be sure he was safe.

So for ten minutes she walked and watched him, and everything was fine, and she began to think about the food and St. Mary's church.

But then she saw the three boys at the corner of a quiet back alley[1], and she suddenly felt cold.

She knew one of them. The one in the middle. A tall, mean-looking[2] boy with a shaved head[3] called Jimmy.

Jimmy was homeless[4] like Cadha, but that was where their similarities[5] ended. Jimmy was trouble[6], Old Fraser said. A thief, a vandal, and a mugger[7].

---

1 **alley –** *Gasse*
2 **mean-looking –** *aggressiv aussehend*
3 **with a shaved head –** *mit rasiertem Kopf*
4 **homeless –** *obdachlos*
5 **similarity –** *Parallele*
6 **sb. is trouble –** *jd. bedeutet Ärger*
7 **mugger –** *Straßenräuber(in)*

The boy did not seem to notice the three other boys, and for a moment Cadha thought they might not see him. Then one of them said something to Jimmy, and he looked up.

For a second nothing happened, but then Jimmy began to move.

"Oi!¹" he said, but the boy did not seem to hear. "Oi! I'm talking to you. Look at me," he said, but the boy still did not stop. Jimmy then ran over and stood in front of him. But before the boy could scream, Jimmy pushed him into the alley, and the two other boys followed him.

Cadha did not know what to do, but she knew she had to do something, and so she ran to the alley and waited silently behind a large bin.

"Are you stupid?" Jimmy asked, his hand over the boy's mouth. "Nobody ignores me!"

And Cadha could see the terror in the boy's eyes.

"Get his bag," Jimmy shouted, and one of his accomplices² took the bag, and his piano books fell to the floor. "Where's your wallet. Or your phone?" he shouted, and he removed his hand from the boy's mouth.

"My pocket," he said, and Jimmy took them.

"What else? What else have you got?" The boy did not answer, but Jimmy saw a silver necklace³ around his neck. "That. Give me that," he said, but the boy did not seem to hear: he was looking desperately⁴ at the street for help. "Oi, what's wrong with you, are you deaf⁵ or something?"

But the boy still did not seem to hear, and Jimmy laughed.

"You know what, lads, I think he is!" He grabbed his face and moved it so the boy looked at him. "Oi, deaf boy, give me your necklace!"

1   **Oi!** – *He!*
2   **accomplice** – *Komplize, Komplizin*
3   **necklace** – *Halskette*
4   **desperately** – *verzweifelt*
5   **deaf** – *taub*

And this time he understood, but he shook his head.

"No? Then I'll take it off you." And the boy screamed as Jimmy pulled his hair back and tried to take the necklace.

Cadha was tall and well built, but she knew she could not fight all three boys and win. She had to try, though. She had to do something. She remembered a trick Old Fraser had taught her, and she picked up a handful of gravel[1] from the ground. Then she kicked the bin loudly, so that they all turned to see her.

For a second there were expressions[2] of surprise on their faces, but then Jimmy laughed. "Cadha! Get out of it, you rat. This has nothing to do with you."

But Cadha began to walk forwards, looking only at the boy, and as she did so she made three words with her mouth, hoping he understood.

"Ha, look at this, lads. We've got a deaf monkey and a mute[3] monkey. We just need a blind monkey and…"

But Cadha did not let Jimmy finish. She threw the gravel into his face and then turned to hit one of the others.

The boy had closed his eyes like Cadha had told him to, and now he quickly moved past Jimmy to stand with Cadha.

The third boy tried to stop them, but they pushed past him, and in a second they were in the street.

They looked around for help, but there was nobody nearby.

Cadha looked up at the castle, and she knew that they were not far from St. Mary's church.

"Oi!" Jimmy shouted, and he ran from the alley, his eyes red and his face furious[4].

Cadha did not have time to think. She began to run, the boy's hand in hers, and she was relieved[5] to see that he was fast.

But was he fast enough?

1	**gravel** – *Kies*
2	**expression** – *Gesichtsausdruck*
3	**mute** – *stumm*
4	**furious** – *wütend*
5	**relieved** – *erleichtert*

Jimmy and the two others began to chase[1] them, and in a few moments she realised that with the boy she could never reach St. Mary's before them.

She turned into another alley where she knew Jimmy could not see them.

There was a dark doorway near them, and Cadha pushed the boy into it.

"What are you doing?" he said, but she had no time to explain.

She made the shape of two words with her lips.

Trust me[2].

And the boy nodded.

Cadha almost felt happy then, but she knew she had to be quick. She stepped back[3] into the alley and saw Jimmy and the others.

"I'll kill you!" Jimmy shouted, and Cadha smiled because she knew they would all follow her now.

So she ran.

And she ran like a person who knew exactly where to put each foot. Like a person who knew every stone in the city. Every street and every turn.

Because she did. Because the streets were her home, and they were the only home she had.

And finally she reached St Mary's church with its crowd of familiar people in front of it, and she turned to look at Jimmy.

"You're dead, Cadha!" Jimmy shouted, and he moved to take hold of her[4].

"What did you say?" a deep voice asked, and Cadha did not need to turn to see who it was.

---

1   **to chase sb.** – *jdn. verfolgen*
2   **Trust me.** – *Vertraue mir.*
3   **to step back** – *zurücktreten*
4   **to take hold of sb.** – *jdn. fangen*

Jimmy looked at Old Fraser. "This is none of your business, old man. Get lost!"[1]

But Old Fraser did not move, and Jimmy saw the angry faces of the other homeless men turn to look at him.

"I think *you're* the one who should *get lost*, Jimmy. And if I see you around here again there's going to be trouble for you. Do you understand me, Jimmy?"

And Jimmy suddenly looked much smaller. Much more like the boy he was. And he turned around and walked into the night, his eyes still red and sore[2].

A week later Cadha returned to the wall, and she sat and listened to the music like every other week.

Just before nine o'clock the boy began to play the Moonlight Sonata. Cadha saw him look through the window smiling. She saw his mouth form the shape of two words. Cadha thought that she had never felt happier in her life because she understood exactly what those two words were.

Thank you.

---

1   **Get lost! –** *Hau ab!*
2   **sore –** *entzündet*

Edinburgh ist die Hauptstadt Schottlands und seit 1999 der Sitz des schottischen Parlaments. Mit knapp einer halben Million Einwohner ist sie nach Glasgow die zweitgrößte Stadt Schottlands und die Partnerstadt von München. Der größte Anteil der Bewohner sind Schotten, an zweiter Stelle folgen Iren. Wegen der international renommierten Universitäten kommen auch viele Studenten aus ganz Europa nach Edinburgh. Die Stadt ist jedoch nicht nur für ihre Universitäten, ihre Burg und den Whisky (die schottische Schreibweise unterscheidet sich interessanterweise von der in Deutschland verwendeten, die wiederum auch in Irland und Nordamerika üblich ist) bekannt, sondern auch für das Edinburgh Festival. Dieses Festival, das jedes Jahr im Spätsommer stattfindet, besteht aus unterschiedlichen Festivals: Unter anderen gehören ein Film-, Tattoo-, Jazz- und Blues- sowie ein Theaterfestival für Kinder dazu.

7. MURDER IN THE MOONLIGHT

Tony Ricca awoke with a short scream and slapped his naked leg. There was something small and hard on it, but in the pale moonlight that came in through his open window, he could not see what. Perhaps a cockroach[1], or some other insect found in the British Virgin Islands. He hit out again and heard the horrible thing fall to his bedroom floor.

He stretched out[2], rubbed[3] the skin of his leg and was suddenly sure that there was something wrong.

Outside he could hear the gentle sounds of the Caribbean: the crickets[4] in the grass, the occasional car on the distant roads.

Yet his villa was silent, and for some reason this made Tony nervous.

For nearly eleven years he had lived here in Paradise, the name he had given his villa, and at some point in the last six years he had begun to relax. He still had his bodyguards to keep him safe: they walked the walls at night and watched his back in the day. But he no longer slept with his gun under his pillow or worried that Don Leone and his men were coming for him.

Until now.

The villa was silent.

Too silent. Where were the footsteps of his guards on the walls? Their whispers[5] as they shared a joke in the night? The occasional growl[6] of the dogs in the courtyard?

---

1 **cockroach –** *Kakerlake*
2 **to stretch out –** *sich ausstrecken*
3 **to rub –** *reiben*
4 **cricket –** *Grille*
5 **whisper –** *Flüstern*
6 **growl –** *Knurren*

No, something was not right, he thought, and he moved his hand towards the light on his bedside table[1].

"Don't," a quiet voice said, and Tony felt his heart tighten[2] with fear.

In the darkest corner of his room, he heard the metallic click of a lighter, and suddenly there was a flame. Tony saw the face of a man lighting a cigarette, his features distorted[3] in the shadows. Then darkness returned; the only light now visible was the warm orange glow[4] at the end of the cigarette and the pale moonlight from the window.

Tony wanted to shout, but he knew he must not. He did not recognise the face of the man, but he knew that it must be one of his old acquaintances[5] and that waiting and talking were his only chance to see another sunrise[6]. He had money he could use to buy his life. A lot of money. More than most people could imagine.

And then there was the gun. It was not under his pillow any more, but it was not far away; in the drawer of his bedside table.

"Who are you?"

The silent figure did not speak, but Tony saw the glow of the cigarette move, and he knew that the man had made himself comfortable in the armchair.

"Well? Why are you here? What do you want? There are three men outside: all I need to do is shout[7]."

There was the sound of the man taking a long drag[8] on the cigarette. "No, there aren't," the figure said, and Tony knew immediately that it was true.

"Did you kill them? Or pay them?"

---

1   **bedside table –** *Nachttisch*
2   **to tighten –** *zusammenziehen*
3   **distorted –** *verzerrt*
4   **glow –** *Glühen*
5   **acquaintance –** *Bekanntschaft*
6   **sunrise –** *Sonnenaufgang*
7   **all I need to do is shout –** *ich brauche nur zu schreien*
8   **to take a drag –** *(von einer Zigarette) einen Zug nehmen*

"Neither[1]. They're asleep. Your dogs too. A deep, deep sleep. But they will awake in the morning." And the words were said in such a gentle tone that Tony felt a shiver of fear.

"What do you want? Are you here to kill me?"

Did he have a gun? The way the man spoke made him think that he must have one.

"You don't remember me, do you?"

"What? Well how can I? Let me see your face."

There was silence. "Perhaps I will when I finish this cigarette." Tony tried to think. The man's accent was from Chicago, he was sure of that, but there was no trace of Italian there, nothing to make Tony think he was part of the Mob[2].

But he had to be. For eleven years Tony had waited for some wiseguy[3] to find him, to finally get revenge[4] for the way he had handed the old family[5] over to the cops.

"Look, Chicago... That was a long time ago. I had to do what I did. The cops had me, and they knew everything about that fire in the old factory. They said some people got hurt in the apartments next to it and that I would get life[6] unless I helped them. You've got to believe me. They knew everything anyway. They were going to take the old family with or without me." Tony did not like the taste of the words in his mouth. The Mob had felt like a real family to him, and it was only the threat[7] of life in jail that had made him betray[8] them.

"Was it Don Leone? Did he send you? Look, the Don is rich, but I'm richer. I made a lot of money after Leone's men were sent down. Look at me, look at this place. I've got twice what

MURDER IN THE MOONLIGHT

---

1 **neither** – *weder noch*
2 **the Mob** – *die amerikanisch-italienische Mafia*
3 **wiseguy** – *(AE) Gangster von der Mafia*
4 **to get revenge** – *sich rächen*
5 **family** – *Verbrecherbande der amerikanisch-italienischen Mafia*
6 **to get life** – *lebenslänglich bekommen*
7 **threat** – *Bedrohung*
8 **to betray sb.** – *jdn. verraten*

he has. So what's he paying you? Because whatever it is, I can double it."

Tony tried to sit up[1], but he was suddenly aware of a pain in his leg, and he stretched out to rub it.

The figure in the dark took another long drag on the cigarette. "You know, Leone said almost exactly the same thing. He thought it was you who had sent me. He was an old man when I went to him. He still spoke like a Don though. At least at first."

"You… Leone, you…?" Tony did not believe it: everyone always said the Don was impossible to kill.

"Why did you call your villa Paradise, Tony? Do you really think you will ever see that place? A man like you?" The cigarette hissed[2] in the dark, and Tony felt afraid now, but he felt something else too. The pain in his leg was worse, the sensation like a burning in his blood, and it seemed to be moving up his body, making his stomach feel uneasy[3].

The gun: think about the gun. You only need a moment. Keep him talking. You have time.

"Did you really kill Leone?"

"Me? No. Killing is for animals."

"So he's not dead?"

"Oh, he is. He died quickly and in pain. For a while he did not even realise he was dying. How do you feel, Tony?"

"What?" And now he could feel it. Something in his stomach. Something in his body. He tried to move, but his legs felt heavy and useless. "What have you done to me?"

The light of the cigarette burnt again. "Me? Nothing."

The gun. Get the gun. Shoot him.

There was a gentle laugh, and Tony saw the figure rise and walk to the window, the cigarette still burning slowly in his hand.

---

1 **to sit up** – *sich aufsetzen*
2 **to hiss** – *zischen*
3 **uneasy** – *mulmig*

In the pale moonlight Tony could now see the man's face. There was a horrible scar[1] on his cheek that went around his mouth and up to his eyes, and there was no hair on the left side of his head.

"Who are you?" Tony asked again, but he thought that maybe he knew now.

"I saw you testify[2] against Leone. I was waiting for revenge, but I never found it. The police never gave it to me. They sent your boss, the one who told you to burn the factory, to jail, but that wasn't enough. And they gave you your freedom: freedom to hide here."

For a moment there was silence, apart from the gentle sound of the waves outside and the steady hum of the crickets.

"I never found my revenge, until now. I discovered your villa a year ago. I could have killed you then[3], but I needed to decide how. Sally died in a very bad way, screaming as the flames took her. I wanted your death to be like hers." "Sally?" Tony tried to move his hand to the drawer where the gun was, but his arms felt useless, and the pain in his leg was growing. "I don't know what you mean... I..."

"Yes you do," the figure said, and the scarred figure turned.

Tony tried to roll over[4], but now the burning pain was in his chest and his arms. "What have you done to me?" he screamed.

The figure turned. "First tell me what you did."

Tony hesitated[5], but only for a moment as the pain was too much. "Okay! The factory, the fire. But, I just did what Leone told me. I didn't know anyone would get hurt."

"But they did!" the figure shouted, and he stepped forward, his eyes full of anger. "Sally! My wife! We lived in the apartment next to the factory. I couldn't save her. You animals killed her!"

MURDER IN THE MOONLIGHT

---

1   **scar –** *Narbe*
2   **to testify –** *aussagen*
3   **I could have killed you then. –** *Ich hätte dich dann umbringen können.*
4   **to roll over –** *sich umdrehen*
5   **to hesitate –** *zögern*

And the figure raised his hand, and for a moment Tony thought he was going to hit him.

Instead the figure held up the cigarette, which was almost finished. "Look Tony, no more time," he said and dropped it on the floor.

"What do you mean no more time?" Tony asked, but then the pain seemed to reach his heart, and he screamed. "It's burning! Help me! It's burning!"

The figure laughed gently and picked something up from the floor.

"What… what is that? What have you done to me?" Tony shouted.

The figure held up the strange shell, and Tony saw something wet retreat[1] inside. "For a year I sat and watched you Tony, thinking about how to get my revenge. Then, one day I heard of a man who was killed by one of these. Its proper name is 'Conus geographus'[2], and it's a type of snail[3]. It's an animal, like you. And a killer. Like you. It has a single tooth in its head, and it uses it to kill fish. It paralyses them and the venom[4] burns inside them, and then within a few minutes they die."

"Help me… I have money… hospital, please!" Tony tried to say.

"Too late, Tony. Do you know what some people call this creature? The 'cigarette snail.' Do you know why? Because after it bites you have just enough time to smoke a cigarette before you die," the figure said, and he looked once more at the now motionless[5] Tony Ricca. "So I smoked it for you."

1	**to retreat** – *sich zurückziehen*
2	**Conus geographus** – *Landkartenkegel*
3	**snail** – *Schnecke*
4	**venom** – *Gift*
5	**motionless** – *regungslos*

Die Britischen Jungferninseln (**British Virgin Islands**) sind ein britisches Überseegebiet in der Karibik. Die offizielle Sprache der über 60 Inseln ist Englisch. Bis auf die Insel Anegada handelt es sich um Vulkaninseln, wo ein tropisches und feuchtes Klima vorherrscht. Bereits seit dem 1. Jahrhundert v.Chr. sind die Inseln von den Arawak bewohnt. Nachdem Christoph Kolumbus die Inseln 1493 für die Europäer entdeckte, begann ein jahrhundertelanger Kampf, der schließlich 1672 mit der Annektierung durch England endete. Damals konzentrierten sich die Engländer auf den Zuckerrohrbau, zu dessen Zweck sie zahlreiche Sklaven schwarzafrikanischer Herkunft einfuhren. Bis heute ist der Großteil der Bevölkerung afrikanischer Abstammung.

8. THE LADY'S SLIPPER

The day was bright and sunny, and a cool breeze drifted[1] across the green grass of the Silverdale golf course[2].

All of the golfers agreed that it was a day with perfect golfing conditions, the mood on the course was good and there were smiles on nearly all of the faces of the men and women there.

But not on *all* of the faces.

Two men stood quietly under the shade of a tree near to the first pin[3] and looked around. They did not smile, and they did not seem in any hurry[4] to start their game.

"I feel like an idiot," said one, his London accent very different to the Lancashire accents of the golfers of Carnforth. "And I hate the north of England. What are we doing here, Den?"

"You know what we're doing here, Billy. A job for the boss. And you are an idiot, with or without those golf clothes."

Den did not hate the north. He was a Londoner, like Billy, but he had always enjoyed the countryside, and he had been impressed by the hills and valleys on the journey from London.

"I mean, it's well grim[5]. There's nothing here, just hills."

Billy was tall and well-built, his head the shape of a brick and probably just as hard[6]. He was useful to have around normally, but not for this type of job. This one required[7]

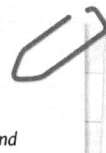

1   **to drift** – *wehen*
2   **golf course** – *Golfplatz*
3   **pin** – *Flaggenstock*
4   **to be in a hurry** – *es eilig haben*
5   **well grim** – *(Cockney-Dialekt) deprimierend*
6   **just as hard** – *genauso hart*
7   **to require** – *erfordern*

patience, intelligence, skill[1]. All things which Den knew that Billy did not have.

"Look, just keep your mouth shut, and do what I say, and we can be out of here in no time[2]."

Billy looked annoyed. "Alright, don't get all Punch and Judy[3]."

"And stop that, too."

"What?"

"The Cockney rhyming slang. If you have to speak, then don't do that."

"Why not?"

"Because we're supposed[4] to be golfers: we're supposed to be rich bloody golfers. That's why we're dressed like this."

"What, and all golfers speak like posh prats[5] do they?"

"Excuse me, can we play through?" a posh voice said from behind them, and they turned to see two middle-aged men waiting.

"Er, what?" Den said, not understanding

"Can we play through? You know, cut in front of you[6]. If you aren't ready."

"Er, yeah." Den said, and the two golfers looked at them suspiciously before quickly hitting their balls onto the course and walking away.

"See! You see that? The way they looked at us. The boss told us not to attract attention." Den shook his head. "Come on, we should start: we look strange standing here."

But for a moment they both stood there.

"What? Me first?" asked Billy. "I don't know how to do this!"

"You're an idiot: all you have to do is hit it."

1	**skill** – *Geschick*
2	**in no time** – *im Nu*
3	**Punch and Judy** – *(Cockney-Dialekt) mürrisch*
4	**to be supposed to** – *eigentlich sollten*
5	**posh prat** – *vornehmer Trottel*
6	**to cut in front of sb.** – *sich vor jdn. drängeln*

Billy put a ball down, pulled a club[1] from the golf bag and looked at it. "Stupid game. Look at that ball: it's too small."

"Right. Give it to me," Den said, and he took the club, and stood in a position similar to that of the two men.

Then he swung[2].

And he hit the floor.

"Alright, let's go," he said, and he tried not to listen to Billy's laughter.

They walked for five minutes, and Den tried to remember the map of the course and the location of the thing that they had to steal.

"It's priceless[3], Den, do you understand?" the boss had said. "There's a collector[4], a German, and he has made an offer to anyone who can get it for him. So you have to get up there quickly, because more people are interested. Oh, and Den, he's only going to pay if it's in one piece, so no funny business[5]. Get it nice and quietly, in one piece, or maybe you should think about staying up there. Understand?"

So here they were, and they were near to it now. Yes, it should be somewhere behind those trees to their left.

"Did you bring the tools?" he asked Billy.

"Yeah, they're all in the golf bag."

Den kept walking[6] and opened the pocket at the side of the bag. Inside there were two hand shovels[7], a large plastic bag, some cable cutters and something which Den had not expected to see.

"What the hell is that?"

"It's a gun, isn't it?"

1	**club** –	*Schläger*
2	**to swing** –	*zum Schlag ausholen*
3	**priceless** –	*unbezahlbar*
4	**collector** –	*Sammler(in)*
5	**no funny business** –	*keine Dummheiten*
6	**to keep doing sth.** –	*etw. weitermachen*
7	**shovel** –	*Schaufel*

"Did I tell you to bring a gun?"

"No, but we're in the north; you don't know what could happen up here, do you?"

"Idiot. We're on a bloody golf course."

"Yeah, well, you didn't tell me what we were gonna steal."

And it was true, Den had not told Billy exactly what the plan was, but only because he knew Billy would complain.

"It's called the lady's slipper, or *Cypripedium calceolus*."

"What the hell's that then? Some kind of drug?"

"On a golf course? Don't be an idiot."

Den stopped near the trees and looked up. There was a CCTV camera[1] on a high post[2] that was pointed at exactly where he wanted to go, but he had planned for this. All he needed was five minutes. If they cut the power[3] to the camera, that should give them enough time to get it. Then, if anyone tried to stop them getting out, well, Billy could resolve that problem.

"Billy, go cut the wire[4] to that camera; then come find me[5] behind the trees."

He looked around once. There were two men, perhaps golfers, walking in their direction; however, there was something strange about them.

But he had no time to wait, Billy was already at the camera, and he had the cable cutters in his hand.

It had to be now, so Den walked to the trees, the golf bag on his shoulder. For a few seconds he saw nothing but green and brown leaves and long grass, but then he saw it.

A splash of colour. Purple and yellow.

And for a moment Den stopped and looked at it, and he forgot that he only had five minutes; he forgot how angry the boss would be if he didn't do the job.

---

1 **CCTV camera** – *Überwachungskamera*
2 **post** – *Pfosten*
3 **to cut the power** – *den Strom abstellen*
4 **wire** – *Kabel*
5 **come find me** – *komm zu mir*

He just looked at it.

"A flower? Are you pulling my leg[1]? It's just a flower?" Billy said as he saw it.

"No, not just a flower. This is the only orchid of this type in the whole of Britain. It's been here for more than a hundred years. It's… it's priceless."

"What do you mean priceless?"

"I mean a single cutting from this plant is worth five grand, but the whole thing is worth a fortune[2]."

"Five grand? Nice one![3]" Billy said, and Den saw him move towards the flower with the cutters in his hand.

"Don't touch it, you idiot. The boss wants the whole thing."

Den dropped the bag and reached for the hand shovels.

"Stop right there," a voice said, and they turned round to see two strangely dressed golfers, one with a gun in his hand.

"Who the hell are you? You're not golfers."

"No we aren't," said one, "and neither are you. Now get away from the flower, or I shoot."

"Bloody hell. They're a pair of thieves like us."

"Yeah, except we have a gun. So get out of here."

Den looked at Billy. Billy looked at Den. They both knew the gun was in the golf bag, and Den's hand was so near to it that he only needed a second.

Billy nodded. Suddenly he shouted, threw the cable cutters and ran towards the two men. Then there was a shot.

Den grabbed the gun from the bag and started to fire. One of the men ran. Billy grabbed the other man and smashed[4] his head into his face, knocking him over[5].

But there was an alarm ringing somewhere on the course now, and Den knew they had to go. "Billy, did he shoot you?"

---

1   **to pull sb.'s leg** – *jdn. auf den Arm nehmen*
2   **to be worth a fortune** – *ein Vermögen wert sein*
3   **Nice one!** – *Nicht schlecht!*
4   **to smash sth. into sth.** – *etw. in etw. rammen*
5   **to knock sb. over** – *jdn. umstoßen*

Billy shook his head then looked at the flower. "Jesus, look what that mug[1] did."

Den looked.

The bullet had cut through the head of one of the flowers, and it was lying on the ground. He picked it up quickly. "Well, it's better than nothing, I suppose. Come on, we need to get out of here[2]."

And they raced[3] through the back of the trees onto a long, open green[4] of the golf course.

Den turned round and saw seven or eight angry golfers run from the trees.

Maybe the one flower was enough, he thought, and he held it carefully in his hand as he ran.

"Are they still coming?" Billy asked, breathing hard as he ran.

Den turned round to look, but didn't slow his speed.

No, it looked like the golfers were just standing and watching them.

"No! Ha ha, we're okay, Billy, just keep running…"

But then something flew past Den's head. Something very close[5] and very fast.

Den turned round and saw something flying in the direction of Billy. He tried to shout, but he was too late, and the thing hit Billy. The big man screamed in pain. "What the hell was that?"

Den thought he knew exactly what is was. He tried to run faster and thought that maybe he would be okay as the car park was just a few metres away.

Then something hit him on his leg, and he screamed too.

"They're bloody shooting at us!" shouted Billy. "How are they shooting at us?"

---

1   **mug** – *Trottel*
2   **we need to get out of here** – *wir müssen abhauen*
3   **to race** – *rennen*
4   **green** – *Grünfläche*
5   **close** – *nah*

"They aren't shooting at us, you idiot: they're just golf balls!"

But then one hit Den right on the back of his head[1]. He ran for another two steps before he realised that everything was becoming black. He felt himself losing his balance, the flower of the priceless lady's slipper still in his hand.

Then, the last thing he saw was the purple and yellow flower being crushed as he fell onto it.

And the last thing he heard was the cheer of the crowd of angry golfers who had decided that enough was enough[2] and that only members should be allowed on their golf course.

---

1 **the back of one's head –** *Hinterkopf*
2 **Enough is enough! –** *Genug ist genug!*

> Der **Silverdale Golfplatz** im nördlichen Stadtteil von **Carnforth** ist tatsächlich einer der letzten bekannten Orte, an dem man die Lady's Slipper Orchidee in Großbritannien noch finden kann. Diese sehr kostbaren Blumen wachsen in versteckten Ecken des Golfplatzes. Jedes Jahr reisen Tausende von Gartenbauexperten und Blumenliebhabern hierher, um sich diese Blüte anzuschauen.

9. THE MAGICIAN

In a small neighbourhood, in a quiet and almost forgotten part of South Boston, Dana Lang looked back at the huge[1] figure of the man who was following her and her boyfriend.

"Does he have to come with us?" she said in an annoyed[2] voice.

Ed Curtis looked at her with an expression that made her instantly change her tone.

"I just mean, it's my birthday, Eddy. I thought it would be just you and me."

Ed shook his head. "Yeah, so it's your birthday. So what? You know I need to be careful around this part of town. There are a lot of people who owe me a lot of money[3]. What do you think? That because it's your birthday, some idiot is not gonna[4] stick me with a knife[5]?"

"But," Dana said, "nobody wants to hurt you, Eddy: you help them, you give them money."

And Ed had to laugh then. The fat around his face moved when he laughed, and he showed his cigar-stained[6] teeth. "Did you hear that, Darius?"

The huge figure smiled.

"Well, you do. You give them money when they need it."

Ed laughed again. Dana wasn't the brightest, but fortunately she was pretty.

---

1   **huge** – *riesig*
2   **annoyed** – *genervt*
3   **to owe sb. money** – *jdm. Geld schulden*
4   **gonna** – *going to*
5   **to stick sb. with a knife** – *(AE, ugs.) auf jdn. einstechen*
6   **cigar-stained** – *gelb verfärbt vom Zigarrenrauchen*

"Baby, I don't give them money, I lend[1] it to them. They need a few hundred bucks[2] to pay the rent? They come to see me, but I'm not Father Christmas. If they want my money, they have to sign a contract that says when they will give it back. And when they give it back, I don't just want a few hundred bucks: I want a grand."

Dana's pretty face looked confused for a moment. "But… what if they can't give you so much money back?"

Ed laughed again. What a dumb broad[3] she was. "If they can't pay, then me and the boys have to go help them think of ways to pay. We take their car, we take their TV, or we make a deal that they give me and the boys what we want, when we want. Have you ever seen me pay for a drink or a meal in this part of town? No. Do you know why? Because I own this part of town. Isn't that right Darius?"

Behind them the huge figure nodded.

"But isn't that, I don't know… illegal?"

Ed stopped walking and looked at her, and he saw the fear appear in her eyes. "What did you say? Illegal? Be careful saying big words like that. This is my town! These immigrants down here… this is not their town. Without me they haven't got anything, so if I want to take something from them, I can."

There was silence for a while as they continued to walk along the street. They could hear the sounds of the seabirds[4] overhead and the sounds from the nearby port where cargo containers were being loaded onto transatlantic ships.

"But aren't you afraid of the police?"

"Baby, the police don't care about these losers. And I'm not afraid of anything."

Dana was silent for a moment, and then she laughed.

1	**to lend sth. to sb.** – *jdm. etw. ausleihen*
2	**buck** – *(AE, ugs.) Dollar*
3	**dumb broad** – *(AE, ugs.) dumme Tussi*
4	**seabird** – *Meeresvogel*

"What?"

"Oh, nothing, Eddy, nothing."

"Are you laughing at me?" he said angrily.

"No, Eddy, it's just, well, I heard you are scared of something."

"Oh, yeah, what's that?"

"Well, someone told me you don't like small spaces like elevators."

Ed stopped again and looked at her. "And who told you that?"

"One of the guys, I think."

Ed looked back at Darius but the huge figure shook his head. "Yeah, well, they were wrong. I told you, I'm not scared of anything. Don't say things like that, they're just lies."

However, it was not a lie: Ed Curtis was terrified[1] of small spaces, and he hated it that someone knew that. He reminded himself to find out exactly who had said it.

"This is it," Dana said, and Ed looked up at the entrance to an old theatre house.

"This, right next to the dock? It looks like a dump[2]."

"But, Eddy, baby, you said I could go anywhere for my birthday, and someone told me this magic show was the best. And it's only here for one night."

"Fine."

"And can you tell Darius to wait here, Eddy? It's not romantic with him around."

"Okay, stay here, Darius. We won't be longer than an hour."

Darius nodded.

Inside the lights were low, and twenty or thirty small tables were positioned in front of a small stage. They found a place in the middle of the room, and Ed looked around to see if he recognised anyone, but the room was too dark.

---

1   **to be terrified of sth.** – *vor etw. entsetzliche Angst haben*
2   **dump –** *Dreckloch*

A waitress took their order[1] and reappeared with two drinks.

"This is going to be great," Dana said, but Ed shook his head and looked at his watch.

"Ladies and gentlemen," a woman's voice said. "For one evening only, you are about to be entertained[2], amazed[3] and confounded[4] by... the amazing Magic Bob!"

Ed shook his head again: what sort of a name was "Magic Bob"?

There was an explosion of smoke and light on the stage, and then the small audience clapped their hands as they saw the magician.

He was not a tall man and not especially impressive[5] either. He wore a simple black suit[6] with a simple black cloak[7], and his dark hair was brushed back over his head.

There was only one interesting thing about him, Ed thought: his large, ironic smile. It looked like the smile of a man who knew something that nobody else did. It looked like the smile of a dangerous cat that was waiting for someone to touch it.

"Ladies and gentlemen, thank you very much," he said. "Now, I am not the greatest magician in the world, but I do have a talent. I can make things disappear!" He smiled again and looked around the room. "Now, who is brave[8] enough to lend me their watch?"

And for the next half an hour the magician displayed a collection of unoriginal but entertaining tricks, and Ed admitted that the man was good.

After some time the magician called for his assistant to bring him the chest[9].

1	**to take an order** – *eine Bestellung aufnehmen*
2	**to entertain** – *unterhalten*
3	**to amaze** – *verblüffen*
4	**to confound** – *verwirren*
5	**impressive** – *beeindruckend*
6	**suit** – *Anzug*
7	**cloak** – *Umhang*
8	**brave** – *mutig*
9	**chest** – *Truhe*

There was silence as the lady pushed something large onto the stage, and the magician uncovered a wooden chest with the word "Tea" printed on the side.

The magician smiled. "Ladies and gentlemen, you see one of the many chests of tea thrown[1] into Boston's harbour during the Boston Tea Party. The Sons of Liberty wanted freedom from their oppressors[2], and so they threw these chests into the sea." There was laughter in the audience.

"Ah, you don't believe me? Well, I assure[3] you that this is one of those chests, and I assure you that it contains magical properties that can help me to make any member of the audience disappear."

Suddenly the lights changed, and only the chest was illuminated.

"Ladies and gentlemen, do I have a volunteer[4]? Someone brave enough to enter this historic symbol of freedom?"

Next to him Ed heard Dana move. "Here, here!" she said, and the lights moved to their table. "My boyfriend Eddy," he heard her say. "He's not afraid of anything."

Ed turned to her with an angry expression, and then realised the entire theatre house was watching him."

"Not afraid of anything? And tell me, Eddy, do you believe in magic?"

Ed looked at the magician and his ironic smile.

"Sure, why not?"

"Excellent! Then please join me!"

Ed walked onto the stage and looked nervously at the chest.

"It's only for a few seconds," the magician whispered in his ear, and Ed nodded.

---

1   **to throw** – *werfen*
2   **oppressor** – *Unterdrücker*
3   **to assure sb. that...** – *jdm. versichern, dass...*
4   **volunteer** – *Freiwillige(r)*

"Now, have we ever met before?" the magician asked, and he placed a pair of handcuffs onto Ed's wrists.

Ed looked at him and shook his head. "No."

The magician smiled and began to tie a rope around Ed's arms. "And do you know anyone here in the audience?"

"Just my girlfriend Dana," he said, and the magician smiled again and quickly tied his legs.

"Only Dana? Are you sure?"

And the lights changed again. Ed blinked[1] as suddenly the whole room was illuminated.

For a few seconds he could not see anything, and he did not know why the music had stopped and why the audience was silent.

But then he could see again, and he looked around the room at thirty angry and silent faces.

A second later he realised he recognised those faces.

"Hey, what is this?" he said, and he began to remember why he recognised the people.

They were his clients: the losers who owed him money.

The losers who hated him.

Ed Curtis opened his mouth to shout for Darius, but the magician pushed a red cloth into it.

"Now ladies and gentlemen, my final trick is to make this horrible little man and all of your money problems disappear. Can I have a beautiful assistant from the audience? Dana?"

Ed watched in horror as his girlfriend walked confidently[2] onto the stage with a large smile on her face.

"Can you open the chest please, Dana?"

---

1   **to blink** – *blinzeln*
2   **confidently** – *selbstsicher*

"With pleasure¹," she said, and she whispered something in Ed's ear. "This is what you get for treating my family like you own them, you creep²."

The magician pushed Ed back, and he fell into the chest. He heard the cheer of the audience, and then the lid closed.

"Okay, let's get this to the dock. It's booked on a ship to Australia!" the magician said, and there was another cheer.

Then suddenly there was silence in the theatre house, and Ed heard a familiar voice.

"Where's Mr Curtis?" said Darius' deep and unintelligent voice, and Ed Curtis felt hope fill him.

There was a second of silence, and the lights faded. Then the music began again, and Ed heard the magician move to the front of the stage.

"Well, good evening sir. Tell me, do you believe in magic?"

---

1   **with pleasure –** *gerne*
2   **creep –** *Widerling*

Boston liegt in Massachusetts, an der nordamerikanischen Ostküste und ist die größte Stadt Neuenglands. Eines der bekanntesten Ereignisse in der Geschichte der Stadt ist die sogenannte Boston Tea Party, die sich im Jahre 1773 zugetragen hat. Einige Bostoner, die sich als Ureinwohner verkleidet hatten, verschafften sich damals Zugang zum Hafen und warfen etliche Kisten Tee, die britische Schiffe geladen hatten, ins Wasser. Diese Zerstörung britischen Eigentums bildete den Höhepunkt eines Streits um Steuer und Zölle zwischen den amerikanischen Kolonien und Großbritannien, der letztlich weiter eskalierte und zum Unabhängigkeitskrieg führte. Die heutige konservative US-amerikanische Tea-Party-Bewegung hat sich nach diesem berühmten Ereignis benannt, da sie sich ebenfalls unter anderem gegen Steuererhöhungen einsetzt.

10. THE END
OF THE LINE

"You've got about two minutes to explain to me what the hell you're doing in my house, and then, if I don't like the answer, I'm gonna shoot you in the head. Does that sound fair enough to you?"

Liz was on the floor, and the rifle of the woman was pointing directly at her.

She could lie, she knew, but if she was about to die in this cold, damp[1] cellar, she wanted her last words to be the truth.

"Okay, but can I stand?"

The woman, who was tall and broad[2], laughed. "You stand up, and I shoot. You try anything stupid, and I shoot. Now talk."

Liz nodded.

It was a short story, and simple.

"I work for the phone company. I repair the lines when there's a problem. I work all over the Northern Territory, from Katherine to Nhulunbuy to here at Roper Bar. The main office is back in Darwin. Look, I have a business card." She started to look in the pockets of her brown khaki uniform, but the woman shook her head. "Just keep your hands where I can see them."

Liz stopped searching, but she knew now that her screwdriver was still in her pocket. She knew that she had a weapon to defend herself with.

"The storm a couple of days ago caused problems with heaps[3] of phone lines. For the last couple of days my partner and I were driving all over the place trying to repair them."

---

1   **damp** – *feucht*
2   **broad** – *breit gebaut*
3   **heap** – *ein ganzer Haufen, sehr viele*

"Your partner? You got someone else here?"

"No, he hurt his hand last night. He drove back to Katherine this morning to see a quack[1]. I've been working by myself all day. Then, about an hour ago, I was thirty miles down the road. There's a section where a couple of telephone lines meet, and it was a bloody mess[2] after the storm. I was on the ladder for two hours, and it was getting dark. I knew I had to finish for the night, but I wanted to see if everything was working."

Liz moved a little, just enough so that she could more easily reach the screwdriver.

She wondered if her leg was okay. The woman had hit her on the back of the head, and she had fallen. There was blood on her left knee, but she thought she could probably stand on it.

"Keep talking!" the woman said.

"I attached the handset[3] to the line. I wanted to see if I could connect to Roper Bar, but there was nothing. A dead line we call it. So I used my screwdriver to move it around, and that's when I heard it."

"Heard what?"

"Don't you know?"

"How the hell would I know[4]? Don't play games with me."

Liz watched her carefully: either she was telling the truth, or[5] she was very good at lying.

"I heard a kid's voice. A little boy."

The woman's eyes narrowed[6].

"He was talking quietly, like he wanted someone in the building not to hear him. He was asking for someone to help him: for someone to call the police. He said his name was Jacky, and he didn't know where he was. He said that someone had

THE END OF THE LINE

---

1 **quack** – *(AUS, ugs.) Arzt*
2 **mess** – *Durcheinander*
3 **handset** – *Hörer*
4 **How the hell would I know?** – *Woher zum Teufel soll ich das wissen?*
5 **either... or** – *entweder... oder*
6 **to narrow** – *sich verengen*

taken him and that he wanted his mum. I tried to speak to him, but he couldn't hear me."

Liz stopped talking.

If this woman had taken the little boy, if she was the kidnapper, then she would probably shoot her now. And if that was going to happen, Liz did not want to be lying on the floor when she died.

"I'm going to stand up now, but I'm not going to move, so don't shoot me, alright?"

The woman did not say anything as Liz rose, but neither did she shoot.

"I don't know what kind of story you're telling, but I don't see how it answers the question of what you're doing in my bloody cellar."

"I didn't know where the call was coming from. All I knew was that it had to be from the north, because the line to the south was dead. I didn't know what to do. Maybe I should have gone for the cops, but I didn't. I got in my truck, and I followed the telephone lines. I passed three other houses; all were empty. Then I got here, and I saw the lights. I looked at my map, and you know what? This is the last house. After this, there's nowhere to go. So I saw the cellar window, and I climbed in."

The woman seemed to move the gun in her hand. Liz thought it was her last chance, and she was about to reach for the screwdriver when the woman spoke.

"You broke into my house, into my cellar, because you thought there was some kid in here? That I was some kind of criminal?"

"Yeah. And that's when you hit me on the head and started pointing that gun at me."

For a second there was silence in the cellar. The woman looked angry but uncertain too.

"Jesus," she said. "I think you're telling the bloody truth." And she lowered the gun.

Liz felt her legs go weak. "You mean, the kid, he's not..?"

"Of course he's not bloody here. But if some sicko[1] has got a little kid somewhere, we need to call the cops, now!"

Liz shook her head. "The line's dead, I told you. There's nothing I can do to repair it."

"Christ![2] Then we drive for help. Ropers Bar is small. There's no cop shop[3], but we can tell the locals to send someone to Katherine for the police. Get a search party[4] out to look. Come on!"

"What's your name?" Liz asked as she quickly followed the woman up the stairs.

"Bess," the woman said and stopped near the front door. "And look, I'm bloody sorry that I hit you, but you were in my bloody cellar like some sort of thief."

"It's okay. I would do the same thing if I was alone out here in the middle of nowhere."

"Yeah," Bess said as they stepped out into the dark. Then she stopped and turned to Liz with a strange expression on her face. "What did you say before?"

"What? When?"

Bess looked north. "Struth![5] You said that the call came from the north, that you looked on the map and that this was the last house. That there was nowhere else to go."

"This *is* the last house."

"Yeah, on the map maybe, but there *is* another place! An old telegraph building, and the phone line connects to it."

"How far?"

"Ten minutes down the road, and then up the old track. Come on! We can take my truck."

The drive was fast and dangerous, and Bess drove like someone who knew that something terrible was about to

---

1   **sicko** – *Geistesgestörte(r)*
2   **Christ!** – *Um Gottes willen!*
3   **cop shop** – *(AUS, ugs.) Polizeiwache*
4   **search party** – *Suchtrupp*
5   **Struth!** – *(AUS, ugs.) Mensch!*

happen. "That poor kid," she kept repeating. "If someone has hurt a kid, I'll bloody kill them!"

Finally they reached an old abandoned[1] building, and Bess stopped.

"Did you see that?" Bess asked. "I think I saw a light in the upstairs window.

Liz looked up, but saw nothing.

"Come on!" Bess said urgently[2]. "We need to find that kid. You go in the front; I'll go round the back." Then Bess looked at her. "Do you have anything? A weapon? I mean, the kidnapper could still be there."

For some reason Liz thought about lying for a moment: there was a strange feeling in her stomach – a doubt. But then she took the screwdriver from her pocket and showed it to Bess.

"Well, it's not much, but it's something. If you see anyone; if you need help, just shout and I'll be there."

They got out of the car and without another word Bess disappeared into the darkness.

Liz was alone, the empty telegraph building in front of her, the screwdriver in her hand.

Everything was happening so quickly.

Was it doubt in her stomach, or just fear?

She walked quietly to the door of the building and pushed it open. Inside it was silent and dark, but she could smell matches or candles in the air.

She pulled a small torch from her belt and shone it around[3]. There was no one there, but in the corner of the room there was a broken telephone on the floor.

This is the place, she knew, and she turned the torch to the stairs and slowly began to walk up them.

She had reached the final step when she heard it.

---

1 **abandoned –** *verlassen*
2 **urgently –** *dringend*
3 **to shine the torch around –** *mit der Taschenlampe die Gegend ableuchten*

A slight[1] sound. Something muted[2] and almost impossible to hear.

Bess had told her to shout, but what if there was someone else in the house?

Or what if Bess was the person who had taken the boy? What if everything she had said was to get her here to this dark, empty place?

She turned to her left. In the darkness she could see a closed door, and it looked like someone had very recently been through it.

She took the screwdriver in her hand and pushed open the door.

The room was black, and it was almost impossible to see, but there, in the middle of the room, illuminated[3] by the moonlight, was a small boy tied to a chair.

He was kicking his feet and trying to shout, but there was a gag[4] in his mouth. For only a second Liz hesitated, and then she ran into the darkness.

She had almost removed the gag when she heard the noise behind her, and she saw Bess standing in the doorway, the rifle in her hand.

"Help me!" Liz shouted.

But the other woman did not step into the room.

She raised the rifle.

Liz saw the crazy, angry look in the other woman's eyes.

No! She thought, but she had no time to speak.

The sound of the shot exploded in the darkness.

For a second Liz did not know what had happened. She could not hear, her ears filled with the sound of the explosion.

1   **slight** – *kaum vernehmbar*
2   **muted** – *gedämpft*
3   **illuminated** – *erhellt*
4   **gag** – *Knebel*

But then Bess put a hand on her shoulder, and she saw the other woman point to the body of the man who had been standing in the dark behind the chair. His dead hand was still holding a sharp knife.

Bess nodded her head and smiled. "Told you I'd bloody kill him," was all she said.

→ Das **Northern Territory** macht mit 224.800 Einwohnern ungefähr ein Prozent der Landesbevölkerung Australiens aus. Die meisten der hier ansässigen Australier leben in der Stadt Darwin, gefolgt von Palmerston und Alice Springs. In diesen drei Städten zusammen leben 80% der Einwohner dieser dünn besiedelten Gegend. Ca. 29% der Bevölkerung besteht aus Ureinwohnern, die seit über 40.000 Jahren hier angesiedelt sind.

11. THE ART OF CRIME

Caroline walked slowly along a wide corridor, past stone pillars[1] and marble sculptures and stopped at a low archway[2]. The crowd behind her followed closely, trying to hear everything she said.

"This section of the National Gallery, ladies and gentlemen, is called the Sainsbury wing. The collection of art[3] kept here is from the Renaissance period and is one of the finest in the world."

She looked at the small crowd as they walked past her. They were the typical Saturday afternoon tourists with faces from many different parts of the world.

"Can I take pictures?" An American woman asked.

"In the permanent parts of the exhibition photography is permitted[4], yes."

"But not in the areas you must pay to see," a quiet voice said.

"Yes, that's correct. In the temporary areas photography is not allowed."

Two Chinese tourists stopped to take a picture by the stone pillars, and Caroline politely smiled to indicate that they must enter the wing.

"We are now going to enter the first room of the wing. The paintings here are some of the most valuable[5] pieces from the Renaissance period, donated[6] to the gallery during the last one hundred years."

---

1 **pillar** – *Säule*
2 **archway** – *Torbogen*
3 **collection of art** – *Kunstsammlung*
4 **to permit** – *gestatten*
5 **valuable** – *wertvoll*
6 **to donate** – *spenden*

She entered the small room with its low roof and nodded to the security guard, Scott, who stood a little straighter and tried to look serious.

Caroline smiled and shook her head at him. He had only been at the gallery for about six months, and he always tried to look serious when the tour groups entered.

"Just don't let them speak to me," he always said. "Or they will discover in two seconds that I have no idea about art."

"You don't need to know about art. Just look after[1] it, and I'll do the talking," she always replied.

Once[2] the crowd was in the room, Caroline got ready to speak. She knew exactly what she had to say and she knew so much about the paintings that she could answer almost any question.

She opened her mouth to begin, but there was a noise from the back of the crowd. Some people turned to look and then a man's voice filled the small space.

"Ladies and gentlemen, the tour is over. I have to ask you all to leave."

"What do you mean?" the American woman asked.

And then they saw him.

He was a tall man with light brown hair and a short, tidy beard. He was wearing a casual[3] cream blazer over a white shirt with blue jeans underneath.

But the only thing that the crowd looked at was the silver gun in his hand.

They screamed.

Caroline watched the crowd fight to get away from the man, and she saw him look at her calmly, the gun not moving from his side. "You can stay for now," he said to her.

"Hey, what is this?" Scott said, and he began to walk towards the man.

---

1 **to look after sth.** – *auf etw. aufpassen*
2 **once** – *sobald*
3 **casual** – *leger*

"Scott, he's got a gun!" Caroline shouted, but the man turned, and Scott froze.

"Get these people out of here, and then lock that door," the man said quietly. "And if you leave, I'll shoot your Renaissance expert," he added in an equally calm voice.

Caroline felt her legs go weak[1], but she was able to remain standing[2], and she tried to keep the fear from her face.

For a few more seconds, the tourists fought to escape from the room. Then Caroline saw Scott by the door. The young security guard put his hand on the door handle[3] and then turned and looked at her.

For a short moment Caroline thought that maybe he would step out of the door and leave her alone with the gunman, but then he slowly closed the door and waited.

"Good. Now come over here next to the brilliant Miss Caroline Stone."

"How do you know my name?" she asked, suddenly more scared.

He smiled and put his left hand into his jacket pocket and pulled something familiar[4] from it. "Because your name is in the museum guide. Miss Caroline Stone PhD. Expert in Renaissance art, especially the Italian masters." The man turned to one of the paintings and pointed at it with his gun. "Tell me, is this from one of the Italian masters?"

Caroline could not stop looking at the gun, but she nodded her head. "Yes, it's by Titian."

"What do you think of his work?"

Caroline was so confused that she could not think, but the words were automatic. "I think that his composition and experiment with form make his work fundamental to the era."

---

1 **to feel one's legs go weak** - *weiche Knie bekommen*
2 **to remain standing** - *stehen bleiben*
3 **door handle** - *Türklinke*
4 **familiar** - *vertraut*

The man nodded. "I agree, but there's something about Titian that I've never liked. Do you know that he was one of the first painters to have international clients? I sometimes think that the problems that the art world now faces[1] started with him. It's not art when you start to sell and buy, when you make people pay to see these masterpieces[2]. No, when you do that, it's just one thing, Caroline. It's just business."

He turned and looked at her, and she saw that his light blue eyes were clear and intelligent. "Caroline, if I don't get what I want today, I believe that this Titian will be my first victim. I want you to think about that."

"What do you mean?"

"I mean, soon the police will be here, and I'll need hostages[3] if I want them to give me what I want. I need you to go to them, to convince them that I'm serious. Do you believe that? That I'm serious?"

Caroline nodded.

"Good. Then, you see, when I release[4] you, I will only have the security guard, and I don't think the police will give me what I want if all I have to offer them is the life of one man."

Scott put his face in his hands, and the gunman smiled. "Please, don't worry. Caroline is going to get exactly what I want. And if she does, there will be no reason for me to kill you. And there will be no reason for me to destroy any of these priceless paintings."

"But…" Scott managed to say. "Who are you? What do you want?"

The gunman smiled. "What an excellent question. Well, I could lie and give you a fake[5] name, but I hate fakes. I hate fake people, and I hate fake art. Burn it all, I say," and he

---

1 **to face a problem** – *vor einem Problem stehen*
2 **masterpiece** – *Kunstwerk*
3 **hostage** – *Geisel*
4 **to release** – *befreien*
5 **fake** – *falsch*

smiled again. "And there really is no reason for me to lie. Your security cameras can see me, and the police are probably trying right now to discover my identity. So let me make a proper introduction. My name is Richard Marx. I am an art enthusiast, and I'm here because I want to give this art back to the people, to liberate[1] it from the constrictions[2] of capitalism."

Scott shook his head. "I don't understand."

"Of course you don't. But maybe our expert will. Caroline?"

"Liberate the art? The gallery is free. Anyone can enter, and anyone can see these paintings."

"No. That's not true, Caroline. Only some of the art is free. There are other exhibitions where the public must pay."

And Caroline remembered the voice from the crowd as they entered the Sainsbury wing.

… not in the areas you must pay to see…

She knew that it was the gunman who had spoken.

"It's true that for some exhibitions there's a small fee[3]. But the money is used to hire[4] some of the pieces from other countries or to help with restoration and conservation or…"

"Enough!" Richard shouted, and for the first time the gun pointed at her.

"Hey, you don't need to do that," Scott said.

Richard smiled, nodded his head and let the gun move back to his side. "No, that's true. I apologise. The subject is something that makes me quite… passionate[5]." He looked at Caroline. "But what you say is not true. The money that is taken from the public goes into the pockets of the capitalists. And I've had enough, Caroline. They can control the business world, they can control the political world, but they can't control the art world." He stopped and looked at the Titian painting again, and then

---

1 **to liberate** – *befreien*
2 **constriction** – *Beschränkung*
3 **fee** – *Gebühr*
4 **to hire** – *mieten, ausleihen*
5 **passionate** – *leidenschaftlich*

he looked at his watch and nodded his head. "And this is why I must ask you to leave us, Caroline, because the police will be here now, and you're going to ask them for something."

"What?"

"Twenty million pounds."

There was silence in the exhibition room.

"Twenty million pounds?" Caroline finally managed[1] to say.

"That's correct. It's an amount[2] that I have very carefully chosen. It is only a small percentage of the price of the many valuable paintings in this room. And it is only a small percentage of the money that this gallery has taken from the public to show the art that belongs to us all. But it is a fair amount, I believe."

Caroline shook her head, but Richard moved near to her and put his left hand on her arm.

"Go now," he said, "and tell them everything that I have said. The money must be transferred directly into this account," and he held out[3] a piece of paper for Caroline to take. "Only when I see that the transfer is complete, will I let Scott go. And remember, our security guard friend is not my only hostage. In the next few minutes, Scott and I are going to place[4] small explosives onto the frame[5] of each of these paintings. If anyone tries to enter this room, if the door opens, the explosives will detonate and destroy these masterpieces completely."

"You can't do that!"

"Why not? It's not their art. It's ours, the public's, mine. And if they give me the money, I won't. It's just business Caroline. It's just like what the gallery does. If they want to see the paintings again, they have to pay. It's just business."

Caroline looked at Scott, but the security guard was frozen with fear.

---

1   **to manage to do sth. –** *es schaffen, etw. zu tun*
2   **amount –** *Betrag*
3   **to hold out –** *hinstrecken*
4   **to place –** *legen, platzieren*
5   **frame –** *Rahmen*

"Okay, I can try to speak to them," she said.

"Good," Richard said. "Go now."

She nodded, and she slowly moved to the door, unlocked it and stepped out into the corridor.

"This way, Miss Stone!" a voice commanded, and she saw two police officers in full body armour¹. They signalled her from behind one of the pillars.

The next few minutes were confusion. The police officers took her back to the main² wing of the gallery, and she saw that there were more than twenty other officers waiting in the corridors, each with guns held ready in their hands and armour protecting their bodies.

She was taken through the main building and saw that the police were quickly evacuating it.

When they reached the security office, they stopped, and two detectives in grey suits introduced themselves.

"Miss Stone, this is Detective Blair. I'm Detective Green. We need you to tell us everything that you can about what happened in there."

Caroline looked at the television that showed each individual room of the gallery and saw that one of the screens was not working. "You didn't see him?"

"We did. The camera only just failed³. We think that the suspect is trying to block the signal. We have experts trying to resolve⁴ that now. We saw everything until you left the room, but any information is useful⁵. Here, sit down and have some water."

Caroline sat down on the chair and drank. There were more than twenty people in the small room, and they were all waiting for her to speak.

So she told them everything that had happened.

THE ART OF CRIME

1 **full body armour** - *Ganzkörperrüstung*
2 **main** - *Haupt-*
3 **to fail** - *versagen*
4 **to resolve** - *lösen*
5 **useful** - *nützlich*

"And he says that he wants twenty million pounds, or…"

"We know: we heard that," Green said.

"Are you going to give it to him?"

Blair shook his head. "Only if there's no other option. At the moment we don't know how serious he his. We don't know if the gun is real, or if he has the explosives. Maybe he's just a crazy guy who wants some attention."

"He's not crazy. He's… I don't know… talking sense[1]."

"Do you think he might hurt[2] the security guard?"

"I… I don't know."

"Sir," said one of the officers at the security controls, "the camera is operational[3]."

The small screen was working again, and the black and white picture was visible for everyone to see.

"Jesus, he's really doing it!" Green said.

On the screen Caroline could see Richard and Scott in the room. Richard was pointing the gun at Scott, and the security guard was attaching small black boxes to the frames of the paintings.

"We need to speak to him, to open a line of communication."

"That's impossible from here: there's no sound on this system."

"Then we need to get a phone to him."

"He said if the door opens the explosives will detonate," Caroline warned. "Scott might be hurt, and the paintings. You can't…"

"We have to do something. There are no windows in there. There's no way for a sniper[4] to get a good shot."

"We could cut the lights," Green suggested.

Blair was going to reply, but a phone started to ring and Caroline jumped with surprise.

---

1   **to talk sense** – *vernünftig reden*
2   **to hurt sb.** – *jdm. etw. antun*
3   **operational** – *betriebsbereit, funktionsfähig*
4   **sniper** – *Scharfschütze*

"Miss Stone?"

The phone was in her blazer pocket; but she never carried her phone when she was working.

She put her hand into the pocket and pulled out a small silver mobile. "This isn't mine: he must have put it there."

Blair and Green looked at the screen. Richard had his back to the camera, but he was holding a phone to his ear. "Answer it, and put it on speaker phone[1]."

There was silence in the security office now, and Caroline put the phone on the table and pressed the two buttons.

"Caroline?"

"Yes."

"Are you with the police?"

"Yes."

"Good. When do they think my money will be ready?" His voice was calm and quiet again.

Blair covered the phone with his hand. "Tell him we need more time. An hour."

"Maybe an hour," Caroline said to the phone.

"An hour? No, that's not good enough, Caroline. Did you not tell them that I'm serious? Well, I must give them some proof that I'm very, very serious. The Titian or Scott? Which do you think, Caroline?"

"No you can't! They just need more time."

"You're right. These paintings really are beautiful. I can give them a little more time. But, just so they know that I'm serious…have you attached them all, Scott… yes? Good."

Suddenly they heard the sound of the gunshot[2].

"No!" Caroline screamed. On the small screen she saw blood where the shot had hit Scott in the back, and he fell onto his front and did not move.

"Jesus!" said Blair.

---

1 **speaker phone –** *Lautsprecher*
2 **gunshot –** *Schuss*

"Do we go in, sir?" another officer shouted.

"No!" Green said. "Do not enter that room! We do not have the authority to enter that room and destroy those paintings!"

For a few moments there was chaos in the room, and Caroline began to cry as she looked at the image of Scott's body on the floor.

"Caroline?" Richard's calm voice said on the phone. "Caroline?"

"Shut up! All of you, shut up!" Blair shouted.

"Caroline? Do you think they believe me now? I hope so. Tell them to transfer the money now, or in ten minutes this room and all these beautiful paintings will burn."

Then the phone went dead.

For a moment more there was silence. Then Blair looked at Green. "We need to get the transfer authorised[1]. There's no way out of that room. We transfer the money and then see what he does."

For the next few minutes, everybody was moving and shouting, making phone calls or giving instructions[2].

Only Caroline was silent and still[3].

She sat and watched the black and white image on the screen. She watched the body of Scott lying on the floor of the exhibition room and watched the blood spread out around him.

She tried not to look, but it was impossible.

How could he be dead?

"Sir, we have the authorisation. We can send the money now."

Just an hour ago he was standing straight, trying to look serious.

She looked at the image again, and suddenly a strange thought occurred to her.

---

1 **to authorise –** *bewilligen*
2 **instruction –** *Anweisung*
3 **still –** *reglos*

"Are we sure there's no way out of there?" Blair shouted.

Caroline stood up and moved closer to the screen.

There was something.

"We don't think so. There are some old passages[1] under the gallery. But none of them access[2] that room directly, and it would take him weeks to dig a hole to connect to one of them."

"What's he doing now?"

On the screen Richard seemed to be examining[3] the explosives, but it was not him that Caroline stared at.

There was something wrong.

"Send the money," Green said to one of the officers

"Wait…" Caroline said, but she was too quiet.

"Okay, that's it. Transfer complete."

"No! Wait!" she said more loudly, and Blair and Green looked at her.

"What?"

"There's something wrong with the paintings."

"Caroline, we need you to phone him. Tell him the transfer is complete," Blair said

She stared at the screen and at Scott's body, the Titian, and the painting next to it.

"Oh my God. I don't understand!"

"Caroline, call him."

But then the phone rang, and Blair pressed the answer button.

"Caroline? Or is it the police? Well, that was very quick. I can see that the money is in my account now. And I can only say thank you very much."

"Okay. Now what do you want to do?" Green asked.

"Fake…" Caroline suddenly said, and the room looked at her.

THE ART OF CRIME

1   **passage –** *Unterführung*
2   **to access sth. –** *zu etwas führen, Zugang haben*
3   **to examine –** *prüfen*

"Get her out of here," Blair said quietly.

"Fake!" she shouted. "You fake! You said you hated fakes! You're the fake! Everything you said about capitalism and art and giving it back to the public! You lying fake! You just wanted the money!" she shouted, and ran to the phone.

A police officer tried to catch her, but then they heard laughter, and everyone stopped. "Well done, Caroline! You really are an expert. I never thought you would notice[1]."

"What's he talking about?" Green shouted.

"You never thought I would notice? You idiot! You put the paintings in the wrong place. I moved the Titian last month. It should be next to the Raphael!"

Then they heard someone else laugh, and Caroline understood everything.

"Sorry Caroline. That was my fault. I told you, I have no idea about art. I didn't even notice they had been moved."

"You bastard![2]" she shouted, and then she turned to the detectives. "You need to stop them, now! Open the room!"

"But the explosives?"

"There are no explosives: look at the screen!"

On the screen Richard was standing and looking at one of the paintings. There was no phone in his hand, and he was not speaking.

"Jesus! It's just a video!" Blair shouted. "All teams! Go go go!" he shouted.

And the police pushed past her, and in seconds the room was almost empty.

"Caroline?" Richard's voice said from the phone. "Caroline? I do hope you're not too cross[3]. I mean, no one got hurt, did they?"

Caroline said nothing.

---

1   **to notice** – *merken*
2   **Bastard!** – *Dreckskerl*
3   **cross** – *verärgert*

"And I really do hate fakes, even the ones I make myself. Are you still watching? Any second now, watch."

She looked at the screen and saw Richard move away from the paintings, and after a few more seconds, it happened.

First the Titian exploded, followed by the Raphael and all of the priceless paintings. Flames spread onto the walls, and soon the whole room filled with smoke.

Meanwhile[1], on the floor of the room, Scott's body was still motionless.

"Not too hot for you in there, Scott?" she asked.

The other voice on the phone began to laugh. "That's better! You have to laugh, Caroline. No, I'm okay now: we're in the fresh air. The tunnel from the room to the passage that I have been digging for the last few months was a bit hot, but I guess that's the price of crime. It's behind the air vent[2] where I was standing every time you and your tour groups came into the room. Nothing personal, Caroline. You were just in the wrong place at the wrong time."

"Yes, nothing personal, Caroline," Richard said, and she heard the engine[3] of a car start, and she knew that the police would never catch them now. "It's just business."

THE ART OF CRIME

1	meanwhile – *unterdessen*
2	air vent – *Luftschacht*
3	engine – *Motor*

→ Die **National Gallery** in London enthält eine der umfangreichsten
Kunstsammlungen der Welt mit Werken von van Gogh, Rembrandt,
Hogarth, Monet, Cézanne und vielen anderen Künstlern. Das Gebäude,
in dem sie sich befindet, liegt mitten in der Stadt, am Trafalgar Square,
und wurde 1837 von William Wilkins errichtet. Zwischen 1872 und
1876 wurde ein Flügel an das Hauptgebäude angebaut. 1991 wurde der
Sainsbury Flügel erbaut.

12. **THE BIG FIVE**

The camp fire[1] was high, the night was warm, and the men sitting around the fire beneath the starry[2] sky of the South African plains were drunk.

"We did it![3]" Danie said again, holding his bottle of beer up. "We bloody did it!"

Pete stopped playing the guitar and raised[4] his own beer, but Jan only smiled.

"What's with you, Jan? This is a celebration, man. We did it."

Jan shook his head. "Yeah, we did it."

"What's wrong with you then?"

"Where are Johan and Dawid? They should be here by now," asked Jan.

"Man, they probably stopped for a drink to celebrate," said Danie. "And good for them if they did. Here, have another beer: it's good stuff."

"I don't want any more," Jan said, and he looked into the darkness of the night.

He knew Danie was wrong. Dawid might be stupid enough to stop for a beer, but not Johan. Johan knew what the plan was, and he knew that any delay[5] could mean they missed[6] the plane that was waiting for them a hundred kilometres away.

Pete started playing the guitar again, an old song about a lion following a group of hungry hyenas, slowly waiting for each

---

1   **camp fire** – *Lagerfeuer*
2   **starry** – *sternenbedeckt*
3   **We did it!** – *Wir haben es geschafft!*
4   **to raise** – *hochheben*
5   **delay** – *Verspätung*
6   **to miss sth.** – *etw. verpassen*

to move before it attacked. Jan had heard his old friend play it a hundred times, but tonight he realised for the first time that he did not like it.

"Give it a rest¹, Pete," he said, and the other two looked at him.

"Seriously, relax, Jan. What's the problem?" Danie said, laughing.

"Relax? Don't tell me to relax, you idiot. We still need to get to the plane, to get to Cape Town and get out of the country. And the police are out there, somewhere, looking for us. So don't tell me to relax."

Danie shook his head. "We've got the bloody diamonds, man! This was your plan. Enjoy it."

Jan stood up. He wanted to relax, to think that everything was okay, but he couldn't, not yet. He moved to the jeep and opened the box on the seat. The diamonds inside sparkled in the light of the fire.

"There are more here than we thought. Enough to make us all very rich men. But not if we get caught, Danie. Not if the police find us."

"And how are they gonna do that, Jan? We're in the middle of bloody nowhere. There's nobody for a hundred kilometres!" he laughed, and he picked up another beer and was about to open it when they heard the voice.

"Hello the camp!" someone said from the dark, and the three men froze².

For a moment there was only the sound of the crickets in the grass.

"Jesus! Who's that?" Pete asked.

Jan took the gun from his belt and shook his head. "It's not Johan or Dawid."

"The police?" Danie said, his smile gone.

"I don't know."

---

1 **to give sth. a rest –** *etw. sein lassen, mit etw. aufhören*
2 **to freeze –** *erstarren*

"Hello the camp, I'm coming in."

Jan shook his head. The police would not announce[1] themselves: they would come in with the sirens on and guns firing.

"Who are you?" Jan shouted into the dark.

"A hunter," the man said, and all three turned in surprise. The figure was only a few metres from the fire now, and it seemed like he had moved in a circle around them.

He was a big man, taller than all of them, with large shoulders and a wide chest[2]. He was dressed in dark khaki shorts and shirt, and on his head he wore an old brown hat with a green feather on it.

But Jan focused on his head. Jan knew you could learn a lot about a man from his face. It was the colour of leather, and the large nose was broken and bent[3]. But it was the ice-cold blue eyes and the large scar from ear to neck that Jan found really interesting.

There was a rifle over his shoulder and a large knife at his side, but the man's hands were raised, and Jan saw him look at each of their guns. "Now, you don't need those for me, boys. I just saw the fire and thought I'd see what was happening. A celebration is it?"

Jan put his gun back in his belt but watched the man carefully. "What are you doing out here?"

"Hunting. You?"

Jan was silent, and it was Danie who spoke. "Nah, just a celebration, like you said. We're waiting for a couple of friends."

"Is that right? Well, can I share your fire for a bit? I've got my own drink, a bottle of gin, enough for everyone."

Danie smiled. "Sounds good to me. Take a seat, man."

"Is that alright with all of you?" the man asked, and he looked directly at Jan.

---

1 **to announce oneself –** *sich ankündigen*
2 **chest –** *Brustkorb*
3 **bent –** *krumm*

"Sure, why not?"

The man sat down on the wooden log¹ next to Danie, and Jan took a seat near to the fire.

"What's your name?" Danie asked.

"Herne. And you boys?"

"I'm Danie, this is Jan, and the man with the guitar is Pete."

"Good to meet you all."

"You got a camp near here?" Jan asked.

"Well, I just make my bed where I lie, you know?"

"What you hunting? The big five?"

Herne smiled. "The big five. Well, maybe I am."

"What's 'the big five'?" Pete asked, moving his hand away from his gun and picking the guitar back up.

"Ha! He's a city boy, Herne," Danie laughed. "The big five, you idiot. The animals the real hunters go after. The lion, the elephant, the leopard… I don't remember the others," he said and took the bottle of gin that the hunter offered him.

"The buffalo and the rhino². You can't forget those two. It was a black rhino that gave me this," Herne said, and he lifted a finger to his scar.

"Jesus, man. But you killed it, hey?"

Herne nodded.

Jan saw Herne look in the direction of the jeep.

"Play that song again, Pete!" Danie shouted, and he took another drink of the gin before passing it back to the hunter.

Pete began to play the song about the hyenas and the lion again, the tune³ filling the dark night.

"You want some?" Herne offered, but Jan shook his head.

"You said that maybe you were hunting the big five. What did you mean?" he asked, his hand still near his gun.

---

1   **log –** *Holzklotz*
2   **rhino –** *Nashorn*
3   **tune –** *Melodie*

Herne looked at him. "You know, the Black Mamba isn't black. It's brown or grey. But its mouth, that horrible mouth, that's black. Black as anything you'll ever see."

Jan did not understand. "What does that mean?" His voice was cold and serious, and Danie and Pete stopped to listen.

Herne smiled. "Look, I just saw the light, Jan, and came to say hello. But I should be going now. You keep the gin, Danie." He stood up and he began to walk into the dark.

"What I meant, Jan, was that in everything there is a little truth. The mouth of the Black Mamba is black. I *am* hunting five animals. But the big five? I don't think so."

The man disappeared into the shadows[1], and for a few seconds there was silence.

"Where's he going?" Danie asked, the bottle of gin still in his hand. "What did he mean?"

His question was immediately answered by the sound of rifle fire and the smashing of bone[2], and Jan felt the blood from Danie's lifeless body splash onto his face before his corpse[3] fell to the ground.

"Jesus!" Pete screamed, and he dived next to Jan with his pistol in his hand.

Out of the darkness came laughter. "It's just business, boys. You stole a lot of diamonds two days ago. You stole them from my boss. That was unlucky for you, because I'm just about[4] the only person in this country who could find you this quickly."

Next to him Pete was almost crying. "He's going to kill us, Jan. What are we going to do?"

But Jan had no idea. "Take the diamonds! Take them for yourself. We won't stop you!"

1	**shadows** – *Schatten*	
2	**bone** – *Knochen*	
3	**corpse** – *Leiche*	
4	**just about** – *so gut wie*	

"Do you think you could?" Herne asked, his voice now coming from the other side of the fire, and Jan and Pete turned and fired, the gun shots echoing in the night.

"Did we get him?" Pete whispered. "I think we got him."

Then something flew from the darkness and landed next to them. "I always take a trophy¹, boys. It's habit."

Jan looked at the piece of string² with bone and teeth tied to it, and he heard Pete begin to cry, and he knew why. At the end of the string were two pieces of bone that were still red with blood.   "It's just their finger bones, Pete," Herne said from the dark. "And they didn't feel any pain. They were already dead."

"Johan and Dawid! He killed Johan and Dawid too!"

The laughter came again. "Well, I said I was hunting five animals. Now I have three. I just need two more. So who's next? You know, if one of you runs now, into the dark, I might miss. Or you can wait there for a while, and I can come to you."

He felt Pete move. "No!" hissed Jan. "We need to work together. Attack him."

"What? No we need to go! To run! Come on!"

"Pete no!" Jan shouted.

But Pete was up and running, and for a second there was only the sound of Herne's laughter. Then Jan heard the shot and knew the hunter had not missed.

"Just one left now," the voice from the dark said quietly.

But Jan did not reply. He looked at the bullets in his gun. He had four left. And he decided that if the hunter wanted him, he would try to give him another scar, just like the black rhino had done.

So he waited, and as he waited he began to sing the song Pete had been playing: the song about the lion and the hungry hyenas.

And somewhere in the darkness a now-familiar voice began to sing too.

… And the lion waited for the final hyena to move.

---

1   **trophy –** *Kriegsbeute*
2   **string –** *Schnur*

Das **südafrikanische Flachland** ist eine majestätische, aber auch grausame und brutale Umgebung. Diese Mischung aus Schönheit und Gefahr findet man in vielen Bereichen des Landes wieder, das erst seit 1994 das Wahlrecht für alle Bürger eingeführt hat. Mit dieser grundlegenden Änderung des politischen Systems ging die Apartheid zu Ende. Die großen sozialen Unterschiede in der Gesellschaft sind aber noch immer nicht überwunden. Das hat zur Folge, dass inzwischen viele wohlhabende Südafrikaner aller Hautfarben in sogenannte Compounds ziehen, Vororte, die eine vollkommen eigenständige Infrastruktur haben und rund um die Uhr von Sicherheitsdiensten bewacht werden.

13. THE FUNERAL

"Thanks for coming with me," Mark said as they left the city of Sunnyvale. They were following the other cars along the quiet roads that led to the countryside.

"That's okay," Holly said. "I know he meant a lot to you."

Mark nodded. "Yeah, he was a good man."

The car was hot, and she opened the window, but the warm Californian breeze[1] did not cool her much.

"How far is it?"

Mark pointed to a sign. "About fifteen miles."

There was silence for a moment as Holly enjoyed the feeling of the wind in her short black hair.

"I like your family: they seem nice," she said, thinking about the different people she had met at the funeral[2].

Mark's mother and father had died when he was young, but he had many aunts and uncles and many, many more cousins.

"Yeah, they are. Most of[3] them."

Holly heard the tone in his voice, and she knew that he wanted to say more. They had worked together at the newspaper for almost six years now. He was a good photographer, and she was a good journalist. Now they were good friends, as well as colleagues.

"What is it?"

Mark looked at her, and she could see that he was troubled[4].

"Listen, I know this sounds crazy, but... I don't know.

---

1   **breeze –** *Brise*
2   **funeral –** *Beerdigung*
3   **most of –** *die meisten*
4   **troubled –** *bekümmert*

Something about the way he died feels strange. He was always so fit, so healthy."

"He was old, Mark. You said that in the last year he'd been weak[1] and tired all the time. I just think that's what happens. It was just old age."

"But he wasn't that old, only seventy-eight. A couple of years ago he was fine and healthy. He used to take long walks near the farm and still cycled[2] into town sometimes."

"What did the doctors say?"

"He refused to[3] go to the local hospital, but Aunt Mary made him let the local doctor see him. He visited him maybe six or seven times."

"And?"

"He said what you say: old age. He said Uncle Emit's respiratory system[4] was weak, but there was no cancer, nothing like that."

Holly considered it for a while. She trusted Mark's instincts almost as much as she trusted her own. However, he was upset[5] about the death of his favourite uncle. Probably that was affecting[6] his thoughts.

They drove the rest of the way in friendly silence, and after a while they moved from the main road to a small track.

"Here we are" Mark said, and Holly looked up and saw a beautiful white farmhouse on a small hill.

"It's lovely[7]."

"Apricot Farm. It's been in my family for generations. Some of my happiest memories are the summers I spent here."

1 **weak** – *schwach*
2 **to cycle** – *Rad fahren*
3 **to refuse to** – *sich weigern*
4 **respiratory system** – *Atemorgane*
5 **upset** – *bestürzt*
6 **to affect** – *beeinflussen*
7 **lovely** – *entzückend*

They parked the car next to the many other cars in the driveway[1] and got out.

Holly stopped for a moment and looked up at the three trees near to the garden. "Are these the apricot trees?"

"Yeah. Years ago there were hundreds, but my ancestors[2] started to grow[3] wheat[4] instead, and now those are the only three."

Holly nodded. "Where are the apricots?"

Mark shrugged[5]. "Maybe it was a bad year. Come on, let's go in."

The house was crowded[6] and hot. The family and friends were all talking quietly in their black suits and dresses.

Holly recognised many of the faces but remembered few of the names. An elderly[7] woman with grey hair was offering drinks to the guests, and Holly knew this was Mark's aunt, Mary. Standing next to the buffet were two cousins who Holly had spoken to earlier. Other people smiled sadly at Mark, and Holly nodded politely[8].

For a few minutes they talked to different people, and she was happy to see that Mark was less troubled.

Then a deep voice from behind them spoke, and she saw her friend's face lose its colour.

"Mark?"

"Uncle Pete," he said, and they turned to see a tall elderly man with a white and black beard. "I didn't know you were coming."

"He was my brother."

"Really? And when did you last see him? Did you even know that he was ill?"

1	**driveway** – *Einfahrt*
2	**ancestor** – *Vorfahr*
3	**to grow sth.** – *etw. anbauen*
4	**wheat** – *Weizen*
5	**to shrug** – *mit den Achseln zucken*
6	**crowded** – *voller Menschen*
7	**elderly** – *älter*
8	**politely** – *höflich*

His uncle nodded. "You're angry. You're just like him, you know." Then he paused again. "Emit and I hadn't spoken for many years, Mark, but that was only because he didn't want to speak to me. We had a stupid argument[1], and he never accepted my apology[2]. But he was my brother."

And the older man moved away to speak to someone else.

Holly looked at Mark and saw the anger on his face. "Mark, what is it?"

"Uncle Pete. Emit didn't like him. They had a business together, but something happened, and they split[3] the company." He stopped and thought for a moment. "You know, now Emit is dead, Pete can take control of the entire[4] company. He can double his profits[5]."

Holly shook her head. "Pete, you're not thinking…?"

"I need some air. Are you okay here?"

Holly nodded and watched Mark leave the room.

For a while she talked to some other guests, but then she walked to the back of the house and out onto the porch[6]. She wanted to go look for Mark, when she saw his Aunt Mary arguing with a man with a large stomach at the bottom of the garden. The man seemed worried, and for a while she watched them before she went back into the house.

Thirsty, she went to the kitchen and picked up a glass of water, but it was warm because of the heat.

She looked for the freezer[7] but could not see it. At the back of the kitchen, there was a door to the larder[8], and she pushed it open and enjoyed the smell of the different foods.

---

1   **argument –** *Streit*
2   **apology –** *Entschuldigung*
3   **to split –** *aufteilen, spalten*
4   **entire –** *ganz, gesamt*
5   **profit –** *Gewinn*
6   **porch –** *(AE) Veranda*
7   **freezer –** *Gefriertruhe*
8   **larder –** *Speisekammer*

The freezer was at the back of the room. She picked up a bag of ice and was about to return to the kitchen when she saw something strange.

It was a large bag of something brown and flaky[1]. It almost looked like hard tobacco or crushed[2] nuts. Next to the bag there was a hammer and piece of wood that looked like it had been hit many times. Curious, she put some of the brown flakes to her mouth, but discovered that it had a bitter and horrible taste.

She was about to take a picture of the strange stuff, when she heard Mark shouting in the other room, and she ran back through the kitchen.

"Did you do something to him? Did you? In January he was improving, everyone could see that, but then suddenly this summer he gets worse, and no one knows why? Just tell me Pete. Tell me what you did!" Mark was shouting at his uncle, and the other guests were standing in shock.

"Mark," another voice said, and Holly saw the man that Mary had been arguing with. "You have to believe me, it was a respiratory failure[3]. Your uncle Pete did nothing."

He must be the doctor, Holly thought.

"Mark, you're upset, but you can't say this sort of thing," Aunt Mary said, and she moved him away from the older man.

Holly followed Mark and his aunt back into the kitchen. "Are you okay, Mark?"

He smiled, but he looked pale and troubled.

"He'll be okay, dear. He just needs a cup of tea."

"Can I help?"

"You sit with him; I'll put the kettle on[4]."

For a while she tried to talk to him about something else, but her friend could not forget about his strange ideas.

---

1   **flaky** – *bröckelig*
2   **to crush** – *mahlen, zerkleinern*
3   **respiratory failure** – *Atemversagen*
4   **to put the kettle on** – *Wasser für Tee aufsetzen*

"Aunt Mary, who gets the farm now that Emit is…"

Mary frowned[1]. "Why, dear?"

He shook his head. "Because I need to know that Pete isn't going to live here."

Mary laughed. "Then don't worry. No, Emit changed his will[2] a few months ago. He didn't like our brother, and he would never leave Apricot Farm to him[3]. No, actually, he has left the farm to me, to thank me for helping him this last year."

Mark and Mary continued to speak, but Holly was not listening because she was thinking about an old news story that she had written.

A terrible accident, where a child had been poisoned[4].

She turned and looked at the elderly lady making the tea. She watched her take a silver ball with a delicate metal chain attached to it from the cupboard.

"What's that?" she asked quietly.

Mary smiled at her. "A tea infuser[5], dear. We only like the best tea in this house. Emit liked his tea."

Holly was silent for a second. "Have you lived here for the past year?"

"Yes. Someone had to take care of Emit. He was very weak at the end."

"But Mark said he got better last winter."

"A little better," Mary agreed, and Holly watched her push the brown tea leaves into the infuser.

Holly turned to Mark and shook her head. "I'm so sorry, Mark," she said, and she saw he was surprised at the emotion on her face.

"It's okay."

"No, it's not. You're right, Emit's death *was* strange."

---

1   **to frown** – *die Stirn runzeln*
2   **will** – *Testament*
3   **to leave sth. to sb.** – *jm. etw. hinterlassen*
4   **to poison** – *vergiften*
5   **tea infuser** – *Teeei*

There was silence in the kitchen.

"What do you mean?" Mark asked.

"Do you want to tell him, Mary?"

But the old woman was silent and looked down at the hot water and the silver infuser.

"Mark, your uncle was improving last winter, but only because Mary had no more apricot kernels[1] to crush and put into his tea. Then, in spring, when the trees were heavy with fruit again, she continued her work. I don't know how she got the local doctor to lie: I suppose[2] she paid him. But I think he knows exactly what it was that caused[3] Emit's slow death."

Mark looked at her with an expression of horror[4]. "What? What was it?"

"Cyanide, Mark. Apricot kernels contain cyanide."

---

1   **kernel –** *Kern*
2   **to suppose –** *vermuten*
3   **to cause sth. –** *etw. verursachen*
4   **horror –** *Entsetzen*

> **Sunnyvale** ist eine Stadt im Silicon Valley und somit Teil der
> sogenannten San Francisco Bay Area, die sich um die Städte
> San José und San Francisco erstreckt. Das Silicon Valley ist
> hauptsächlich als einer der weltweit wichtigsten Standorte der
> IT und High-Tech Industrie bekannt. Die Branche beschäftigt in
> Sunnyvale ca. 24.000 Menschen. Das für diese Gegend sehr milde
> Wetter und die trockenen, heißen Sommer mit Durchschnitts-
> temperaturen von 26 Grad ermöglichen den Anbau von Obst und
> Wein.

14. THE ESCAPE

Walt was alone in his cell in Auckland Prison's Delta block when he heard the sound of voices in the corridor.

He was no longer a young man, and his dark hair had turned to grey during the past six years in this small space. But his hearing[1] was still good and so were his instincts. He could sense[2] danger before he saw it, so he moved his hand to his right boot[3] and to the short piece of sharp[4] wood that he kept there.

"Walt?" a voice called, and the old prisoner recognised the deep, mocking[5] tone.

"In here," he said, and he put his hand back on his leg. The voice belonged to a man who could not be stopped by such a small weapon.

Tane stepped into the cell, and Walt took a moment to look at the man. The Maori was massive. Almost too tall to stand in the cell. His shoulders were twice as wide as Walt's and were more heavily muscled than any other man's in Delta block.

But it was the black tattoos on the man's face, head and body that gave him the menacing[6] appearance.

That and his dark, psychotic eyes.

"Walt, my old friend."

Walt nodded, but he hated to hear these words in the Maori's mouth. The idea that he could be friends with this murderer made him feel sick.

---

1   **hearing** – *Hörvermögen*
2   **to sense sth.** – *etw. spüren*
3   **boot** – *Stiefel*
4   **sharp** – *spitz*
5   **mocking** – *spöttisch*
6   **menacing** – *bedrohlich*

"What do you want, Tane?" he said, but he kept the tone of his voice neutral.

Tane smiled, and Walt saw his big white teeth. "I hear that you're leaving us soon."

Walt paused and looked down at the grey stone floor of the cell. "Soon? Yeah. If you think that four years is soon."

"I heard it might be a lot sooner than that, Walt. A lot sooner. Bring him here, Boz."

Boz was Tane's right-hand man, a short, ugly creature with messy[1] blond hair.

Boz pushed a man into the cell and followed him in.

"Chris?" Walt said.

"I'm sorry, Walt, they were gonna break my hands: I had to tell them something."

"He was trying to cheat[2] at cards again," Tane said.

"It's not true, Walt, I swear."

Walt ignored the young man and looked up at Tane. "So he cheated? Why are you telling me?"

"Because the idiot asked us not to break his hands. He said he had some information for us instead[3]."

Walt looked at Chris. He was a tall, thin young man with the face of a boy. People said he was a good thief but that he had met the wrong people and had got involved in[4] a bank robbery where a cop had been shot. For two years he had been in Delta block, and for two years Tane had made his life hell[5].

"I'm sorry, Walt. They hurt me, my hands…"

"Shut it!" Tane snapped[6]. "Boz, watch the door. And whistle[7] if you see a guard."

---

1   **messy** – *unordentlich*
2   **to cheat** – *schummeln*
3   **instead** – *stattdessen*
4   **to get involved in sth.** – *in etw. verwickelt werden*
5   **to make sb.'s life hell** – *jdm. das Leben zur Hölle machen*
6   **to snap at sb.** – *jdn. anfahren*
7   **to whistle** – *pfeifen*

Boz nodded and went to stand in the corridor, and Tane sat down on the chair by the table.

"Now, Walt, you know me. I'm not a bad bloke[1]. But I'm a little bit angry with you. I told you that if you ever discovered a way out of this place, you should tell me, and we would go together."

"What did you say, Chris?"

Tane smiled. "So it's true. You told me there was no way out of here."

Walt shook his head. "There is no way out, Tane: this is maximum security."

"But that won't stop you, Walt. How many prisons have you escaped from? Six?"

"Seven. But they were all medium security."

"Yeah, but I reckon[2] if anyone can get out of here, it's you. And your stupid cellmate[3] tells me you're going to try."

Walt looked into Tane's eyes. The man was a psychopath, but he was not stupid.

If he wanted this to work, he had to be very careful.

"Okay, Tane. There is a way."

Tane grinned[4]. "I knew it."

Walt shook his head. "Look, Tane…"

"No, you look, Walt. I don't know what the plan is, but I know this: Boz and I are coming with you, and that's final[5]."

Walt waited a moment and then nodded. "Okay, but you have to do everything I say."

Tane nodded. "No worries, old man. You're the expert. So what's the plan. When do we go?"

"Tonight. It has to be tonight."

---

1   **bloke** – *Typ*
2   **to reckon** – *schätzen, glauben*
3   **cellmate** – *Zellengenosse*
4   **to grin** – *grinsen*
5   **and that's final** – *und dabei bleibt es*

"Jesus, sweet as[1]! And the plan?"

"Look, to escape from a prison you need five things: opportunity[2], distraction[3], deterrent[4], delay and an exit strategy. Now, we have the opportunity tonight. One of the guards is leaving, and they are having a party for him at the other side of the prison. That means there are going to be fewer guards than usual."

Tane smiled. "Then?"

"Chris works in the canteen[5] in the evenings. He's going to start a fire. That's our distraction. When he does, I know where we can get one of the guard's rifles."

"That's impossible!"

Walt shook his head. "I have a key to the rifle cupboard in the corridor between here and Beta block."

"You have a key? How?"

"The guard that's leaving sold it to me for a small fortune[6]. When the fire starts, the guards will enter through that corridor. I'm going to wait near the door and hope they don't see me. There's only going to be five shots, but it's enough to give us some time and space. That's our deterrent."

"You're a bloody genius, Walt. Then what?"

"Delay. When the guards are in the kitchen, Chris is going to get out and block the doors. It won't give us much time, but enough to get to the corridor that leads to the yard[7]. From there we climb the first fence[8] and get into the exterior space."

"Then what? We can't get over that second fence. It's too high, and there's razor wire[9] all over it."

1	**Sweet as!** – *(Neuseeländisch, ugs.) Cool!*
2	**opportunity** – *Gelegenheit*
3	**distraction** – *Ablenkung*
4	**deterrent** – *Abschreckung*
5	**canteen** – *Mensa*
6	**fortune** – *Vermögen*
7	**yard** – *Hof*
8	**fence** – *Zaun*
9	**razor wire** – *Nato-Draht*

Walt let himself smile a little. "Exit strategy. Do you know who Pascal Payet is?"

Tane shook his head.

"In two thousand and one he escaped from a prison in France, and he did it in a stolen helicopter."

Tane looked at him, and Walt saw the doubt in the man's dark eyes. "A helicopter? Are you telling me someone is going to land a helicopter in the exterior yard?"

Walt nodded his head. "An old friend of mine from the army. At eight."

Tane looked at Walt and then at Chris, who was standing silently in the corner with his hands held together.

Then the Maori grinned, his white teeth looking big and dangerous. "Right then. Boz and I are coming with you, so what do you want us to do?"

Walt shook his head. "Everything is planned. If you want to come, meet us at the corridor to the yard at five to eight. Chris can start the fire and block the guards in the canteen, and I can get the gun."

Tane slapped[1] his leg and laughed. "You're a genius, Walt, my old friend. You get that gun and give it to me, and I will give us time to get to the helicopter."

Walt nodded.

Outside the door they heard Boz whistle, and they knew the guards were coming.

"Chris," Walt said, "you need to get to the canteen."

Chris moved to the door and tried to smile. "You're not too angry are you, Walt? I had to tell them."

"No, Chris, it's okay," he said, and the young man left the cell.

Tane stood up and was about to leave too.

---

1   **to slap –** *klatschen*

"Tane, there's a problem. There's only room for three people on the helicopter. More people means too much weight."

Tane looked angry. "Boz and I are coming."

Walt nodded. "I know, but that means that Chris can't."

Tane smiled. "Fine, we don't need that idiot. So, see you at the corridor. And Walt, I don't want any problems, understand?"

Walt smiled too this time. "I think it's all going to go perfectly."

The sound of the prison alarm and the shouting voices woke Chris up[1]. He was lying on the floor of his cell. The back of his head hurt, and he could not remember exactly what had happened.

Everything had been going perfectly. He had made the fire look like an accident, and in the chaos he had left the canteen and had used three mop handles[2] to block the doors.

Then he had met Walt in the cell, and the old convict[3] had told him that everything was going to be okay and that they had to leave, and Chris had then moved to the door of the cell.

But then something had hit him.

Something from behind him.

Walt…

It must have been Walt.

The alarm continued to ring, and outside there was the sound of chaos.

The escape. Walt had left him here alone. With no protection from the other prisoners. With no friend and no one to help him. And all because he had told Tane about the plan.

"Walt!" he shouted, but the alarm was so loud he knew no one could hear him.

"Yes?" said a voice.

Chris turned his head.

THE ESCAPE

---

1   **to wake sb. up** – *jdn. wecken*
2   **mop handle** – *Wischmophalter*
3   **convict** – *Sträfling*

Walt was standing by the window of the cell.

"You're still here? What about the escape?"

Walt continued to look out of the window. "The plan is working perfectly. I met Tane and Boz at the corridor. I gave Tane the gun then told him I had to go back to block the door to stop the guards. I told him to wait for me in the exterior yard. That's where they are now."

Chris stood up. "But the helicopter… We have to go!"

From outside in the exterior yard there was the sound of gunshots, shouting and two terrible screams that made Chris jump.

"You know," Walt said, turning around and smiling, "I don't think that helicopter is coming, Chris." And he sat down at the table and opened his book.

Chris looked out of the window at the horrible scene and at the two dead bodies.

And he did not understand.

Das **Paremoremo**, wie das Gefängnis von Auckland auch genannt wird, liegt an der Nordküste Neuseelands und enthält den einzigen Hochsicherheitstrakt des Landes. Im Jahr 1993 schafften es Brian Curtis und Michael Bullock nicht nur aus dem Gefängnis auszubrechen, sondern auch für viele Jahre nicht wieder festgenommen zu werden. Seit diesem Ereignis wurden die Sicherheitsvorkehrungen erheblich verstärkt, sodass die Leitung inzwischen behauptet, es sei jetzt ein Ding der Unmöglichkeit, aus dem Gefängnis zu fliehen.

WORTLISTE

Verwendete Abkürzungen

AE = amerikanisches Englisch
BE = britisches Englisch

AUS = australisches Englisch
ugs. = umgangssprachlich

	abandoned	*verlassen*
	access point	*Zugangspunkt*
to	access sth.	*zu etwas führen, Zugang haben*
	accomplice	*Komplize, Komplizin*
	acquaintance	*Bekanntschaft*
to	affect	*beeinflussen*
	agreement	*Vereinbarung*
	air vent	*Luftschacht*
	alley	*Gasse*
	although	*obgleich*
to	amaze	*verblüffen*
	amount	*Betrag*
	amusing	*amüsierend*
	ancestor	*Vorfahr*
	and that's final	*und dabei bleibt es*
to	announce oneself	*sich ankündigen*
	annoyed	*genervt*
	apology	*Entschuldigung*
	archway	*Torbogen*
	argument	*Streit*
	assassination	*Ermordung*
to	assure sb. that...	*jdm. versichern, dass ...*
	ATM	*(AE) Geldautomat*
to	authorise	*bewilligen*
	available	*verfügbar*
	awesome	*(AE) super*
	aye	*(Schottisch) ja*
	bastard	*Dreckskerl*
to	be about to do sth.	*im Begriff sein, etw. zu tun*
to	be in a hurry	*es eilig haben*
to	be supposed to	*eigentlich sollten*
to	be terrified of sth.	*vor etw. entsetzliche Angst haben*
to	be worth a fortune	*ein Vermögen wert sein*
	bedside table	*Nachttisch*
	bent	*krumm*
to	betray sb.	*jdn. verraten*
	bill	*(AE) Geldschein*
to	blackmail sb.	*jdn. erpressen*
	blank	*ausdruckslos*
to	blink	*blinzeln*
	bloke	*Typ*
	body	*Leiche*
	body bag	*Leichensack*
	bone	*Knochen*
	boot	*Stiefel*
to	bow	*sich verbeugen*
	brave	*mutig*
	breath	*Atem*
	breeze	*Brise*
	broad	*breit gebaut*
	buck	*(AE, ugs.) Dollar*
to	bump into sb.	*mit jdm. zusammenstoßen*
	burial stone	*Grabstein*
	camp fire	*Lagerfeuer*
	canny	*schlau*
	canteen	*Mensa*
	capable	*tüchtig*
	casual	*leger*
to	cause sth.	*etw. verursachen*
	CCTV camera	*Überwachungskamera*
	cellmate	*Zellengenosse*

	CEO (Chief Executive Officer)	Geschäftsführer(in)	deceased	Verstorbene(r)

	CEO (Chief Executive Officer)	Geschäfts-führer(in)		deceased	Verstorbene(r)
	change	Kleingeld	to	defend oneself	sich verteidigen
to	chase sb.	jdn. verfolgen		defensively	verteidigend
to	cheat	schummeln		delay	Verspätung
to	cheat on sb.	jdn. betrügen		desperately	verzweifelt
	chess board	Schachbrett		deterrent	Abschreckmittel
	chest	Truhe; Brustkorb		devotion	Ergebenheit
	Christ!	Um Gottes willen!		disguise	Tarnung
	cigar-stained	gelb verfärbt vom Zigarren-rauchen		distorted	verzerrt
				distraction	Ablenkung
				dizzy	schwindlig
to	climb	klettern	to	donate	spenden
	cloak	Umhang		door handle	Türklinke
	close	nah		doorbell	Türklingel
	club	Schläger		doorway	Eingang
	Cockney	Londoner Dialekt	to	drag	schleifen
	cockroach	Kakerlake	to	drift	wehen
	coil of rope	Seilrolle	to	drip	tropfen
to	collapse	einstürzen		driveway	Einfahrt
	collection of art	Kunstsammlung		drug	Medikament
	collector	Sammler(in)		dull	stumpf
to	con sb.	jdn. betrügen		dumb broad	(AE, ugs.) dumme Tussi
	confidently	selbstsicher			
to	confound	verwirren		dump	Dreckloch
	confusion	Verwirrung		dust	Staub
	conservatory	Wintergarten	to	echo	widerhallen
	constriction	Beschränkung	to	edge forward	sich langsam vorwärts-bewegen
to	contemplate	erwägen			
	Conus geogra-phus	Landkartenkegel			
				either... or	entweder... oder
	convict	Sträfling		elaborate	kunstvoll
	cop shop	(AUS, ugs.) Polizeiwache		elderly	älter
				elevator	(AE) Aufzug
	corpse	Leiche		embassy	Botschaft
	corridor	Flur		engine	Motor
	cotton mill	Baumwollspin-nerei		Enough is enough!	Genug ist genug!
	creep	Widerling	to	entertain	unterhalten
	cricket	Grille		entire	ganz, gesamt
	cross	verärgert	to	examine	prüfen
	crowded	voller Menschen		excavation	Ausgrabung
to	crush	mahlen, zerkleinern		exhibition	Ausstellung
to	cut in front of sb.	sich vor jdn. drängeln		expression	Gesichtsausdruck
			to	extinguish	auslöschen
to	cut the power	den Strom abstellen	to	face a problem	vor einem Problem stehen
to	cycle	Rad fahren	to	fail	versagen
	dagger	Dolch		fake	falsch, inkorrekt
	damp	feucht		familiar	vertraut
	deaf	taub		fault	Schuld
				fault in the system	Systemfehler

	fee	Gebühr
to	feel like doing sth.	Lust haben, etw. zu tun
to	feel one's legs go weak	weiche Knie bekommen
to	feel sympathy for sb.	mit jdm. Mitleid haben
	fence	Zaun
	flaky	bröckelig
to	flicker	flimmern
	for	denn
	fortune	Vermögen
	frame	Rahmen
to	freeze	erstarren
	freezer	Gefriertruhe
	fright	Erschrecken
to	frown	die Stirn runzeln
	full body armour	Ganzkörper- rüstung
	funeral	Beerdigung
	furious	wütend
	G'day!	(AUS) Guten Tag!
	gag	Knebel
to	get involved in sth.	in etw. verwickelt werden
to	get life	lebenslänglich bekommen
	Get lost!	Hau ab!
to	get revenge	sich rächen
to	give sb. a slap	jdm. eine Ohrfeige geben
to	give sth. a rest	etw. sein lassen, mit etw. aufhören
	glow	Glühen
	golf course	Golfplatz
	gonna	going to
	grand	(ugs.) Riese, Tausender
	gravel	Kies
	green	Grünfläche
to	grin	grinsen
to	grow sth.	etw. anbauen
	growl	Knurren
	guilty	schuldig
	gunshot	Schuss
	gurney	(AE) Rollbahre
	handset	Hörer
	he would find...	er würde finden...
	heap	ein ganzer Haufen, sehr viele
	hearing	Hörvermögen

to	hesitate	zögern
	hidden	versteckt
to	hide	verbergen
to	hire	mieten, ausleihen
to	hiss	zischen
	hit-and-run accident	Unfall mit Fahrerflucht
to	hold out	hinstrecken
	homeless	obdachlos
	horror	Entsetzen
	hostage	Geisel
	huge	riesig
	humid	schwül
to	hurt sb.	jdm. etw. antun
	I don't think so.	Ich glaube nicht.
to	illuminate	beleuchten
	illuminated	erhellt
	immaculately	makellos
	impressive	beeindruckend
	in fact	eigentlich
	in mysterious circum- stances	unter mysteriösen Umständen
	in no time	im Nu
	in regards to	bezüglich
	inability	Unfähigkeit
	insistent	hartnäckig
	instantly	augenblicklich
	instead	stattdessen
	instruction	Anweisung
to	introduce oneself	sich vorstellen
	jug	Krug
	just about	so gut wie
	just as hard	genauso hart
to	keep doing sth.	etw. weitermachen
	kernel	Kern
to	knock sb. over	jdn. umstoßen
	larder	Speisekammer
to	leave sth. to sb.	jm. etw. hinter- lassen
to	lend sth. to sb.	jdm. etw. ausleihen
	letter opener	Brieföffner
to	liberate	befreien
to	lie back	sich zurücklegen
to	line	säumen
	location	Stelle
	log	Holzklotz
to	look after sth.	auf etw. aufpassen
	lounge	Salon
	lovely	entzückend
	maid	Dienstmädchen

	main	Haupt-
to	make sb.'s life hell	jdm. das Leben zur Hölle machen
to	manage to do sth.	es schaffen, etw. zu tun
	manor (house)	Herrenhaus
	masterpiece	Kunstwerk
to	match	übereinstimmen
	mate	Kumpel
	mean-looking	aggressiv aussehend
	meanwhile	unterdessen
	menacing	bedrohlich
	mess	Durcheinander
	messy	unordentlich
	middle-aged	mittleren Alters
to	miss sth.	etw. verpassen
	mobile (phone)	Handy
	mocking	spöttisch
	mop handle	Wischmophalter
	most of	die meisten
	motionless	bewegungslos
	motionless	regungslos
	mug	Trottel
	mugger	Straßenräuber(in)
	multitude	Vielzahl
	murder scene	Tatort
	mute	stumm
	muted	gedämpft
to	narrow	sich verengen
	nearby	in der Nähe
	necklace	Halskette
	neither	weder noch
	Nice one!	Nicht schlecht!
	no funny business	keine Dummheiten
	nobody but	niemand außer
	none	keine
to	notice	merken
	novel	Roman
	novelist	Schriftsteller(in)
	number plate	Nummernschild
	Oh my gosh!	Oh mein Gott!
	once	sobald
	operational	betriebsbereit, funktionsfähig
	opportunity	Gelegenheit
	oppressor	Unterdrücker
to	owe sb. money	jdm. Geld schulden
	pal	Kumpel
	paramedic	Sanitäter(in)
	passage	Gang; Unterführung
	passionate	leidenschaftlich
to	permit	gestatten
	piece	Musikstück
	pillar	Säule
	PIN	Geheimzahl
	pin	Flaggenstock
to	place	legen, platzieren
	plain	unscheinbar
	pleasant	angenehm
	plot	Handlung
to	poison	vergiften
	politely	höflich
	poor thing	armes Ding
	porch	(AE) Veranda
	posh prat	vornehmer Trottel
	post	Pfosten
	power cut	Stromausfall
to	practise	üben
	priceless	unbezahlbar
	private man	zurückhaltender Mann
	procedure	Standardprozedur
	profit	Gewinn
to	pull sb.'s leg	jdn. auf den Arm nehmen
	purse	Geldbeutel
to	put the kettle on	Wasser für Tee aufsetzen
	quack	(AUS, ugs.) Arzt
to	race	rennen
to	raise	hochheben
	razor wire	Nato-Draht
to	realise	sich klar werden
to	reckon	schätzen, glauben
to	refuse to	sich weigern
to	release	befreien
	relieved	erleichtert
	remain	Rest
to	remain standing	stehen bleiben
	repellent	widerwärtig
to	require	erfordern
to	resist sb.'s charms	dem Charme von jemandem widerstehen
to	resolve	lösen
	respiratory failure	Atemversagen

	respiratory system	Atemorgane
to	retreat	sich zurückziehen
	reverend	Pastor
	rhino	Nashorn
	ridiculous	absurd
to	rise	hinaufsteigen
to	roll over	sich umdrehen
to	rub	reiben
	safe	ungefährlich; in Sicherheit
	sandstone	Sandstein
	sb. is trouble	jd. bedeutet Ärger
	sb.'s legs go weak	weiche Knie bekommen
	scar	Narbe
	seabird	Meeresvogel
to	search	durchsuchen
	search party	Suchtrupp
	secure	fest
	sensation	Eindruck, Gefühl
to	sense sth.	etw. spüren
	shadows	Schatten
to	shake one's head	den Kopf schütteln
	shame	Schamgefühl
	sharp	spitz
to	shine the torch around	mit der Taschenlampe die Gegend ableuchten
to	shiver	erschaudern
	shortly	in Kürze
	shouldn't I...	sollte ich nicht...
	shovel	Schaufel
to	show sb. to the door	jdn. zur Tür bringen
to	shrug	mit den Achseln zucken
	sicko	(ugs.) Geistesgestörte(r)
to	signal to sb.	jdm. ein Zeichen geben
	similarity	Parallele
to	sit back	sich zurücklehnen
to	sit up	sich aufsetzen
	skill	Geschick
	skyscraper	Wolkenkratzer
to	slap	klatschen
	slight	kaum vernehmbar
to	smash sth. into sth.	etw. in etw. rammen

	snail	Schnecke
to	snap	aufschnappen
to	snap at sb.	jdn. anfahren
	sniper	Scharfschütze
	sore	entzündet
	soup kitchen	Armenküche
	speaker phone	Lautsprecher
	splash of colour	Farbklecks
to	split	aufteilen, spalten
	stag	Hirsch
	staircase	Treppenhaus
to	stare at sth.	etw. anstarren
	starry	sternenbedeckt
to	step back	zurücktreten
to	stick sb. with a knife	(AE, ugs.) auf jdn. einstechen
	still	reglos
to	stretch	sich strecken
to	stretch out	sich ausstrecken
	string	Schnur
to	stroll	schlendern
	study	Arbeitszimmer
	subway	(AE) U-Bahn
to	suffer	leiden
	suit	Anzug
	sunrise	Sonnenaufgang
	support	Stütze
to	suppose	vermuten
	Sure!	Klar!
	surely	bestimmt
	suspicion	Verdacht
	sweaty	verschwitzt
to	swing	zum Schlag ausholen
to	take a drag	(von einer Zigarette) einen Zug nehmen
to	take an order	eine Bestellung aufnehmen
to	take hold of sb.	jdn. fangen
to	talk sense	vernünftig reden
	tea infuser	Teeei
	terraced house	Reihenhaus
	terrifying	furchterregend
to	testify	aussagen
to	text	simsen
	text (message)	SMS
	the back of one's head	Hinterkopf
	the most	am meisten
	threat	Bedrohung

to	throw	werfen		vigorously	energisch
to	tie	festbinden		visible	sichtbar
to	tighten	zusammenziehen		volunteer	Freiwillige(r)
	tool	Werkzeug	to	wake sb. up	jdn. wecken
	torch	Taschenlampe		waste of time	Zeitverschwen-dung
to	transfer money	Geld überweisen			
to	trap sb.	jdn. in die Falle locken		weak	schwach
			to	weaken	schwächen
	trophy	Kriegsbeute		What the hell?	Was zum Teufel?
	troubled	bekümmert		wheat	Weizen
	Trust me!	Vertraue mir!		whisper	Flüstern
	tune	Melodie	to	whistle	pfeifen
	uneasy	mulmig		will	Testament
	unremarkable	unscheinbar		wing	Flügel, Trakt
	untidy	zerstrubbelt		wire	Kabel
	upset	bestürzt		with a shaved head	mit rasiertem Kopf
	urgently	dringend			
	useful	nützlich		with pleasure	gerne
	valuable	wertvoll		witness	Augenzeuge
	venom	Gift		yard	Hof
	vertical	senkrecht			

BILDQUELLEN

Umschlag:
Akte: Thinkstock/RTimages; Mondschein: Thinkstock/johnnorth.

S. 15 (Belize): shutterstock/Anton_Ivanov; **S. 22 (Lancashire):** shutterstock/
peter jeffreys; **S. 30 (Houston, Texas):** shutterstock/holbox; **S. 38 (Central
Park):** shutterstock/T photography; **S. 46 (Lake District):** shutterstock/
Ian Duffield; **S. 54 (Edinburgh):** shutterstock/Dennis van de Water; **S. 61
(Virgin Islands):** shutterstock/Dorn1530; **S. 69 (Lady Slipper's Orchidee):**
shutterstock/freya-photographer; **S. 77 (Boston):** shutterstock/Marcio Jose
Bastos Silva; **S. 84 (Northern Territories, Australia):** shutterstock/edella;
S. 98 (National Gallery, London): shutterstock/ Claudio Divizia; **S. 105 (South
African Plains):** shutterstock/Christine Langer-Pueschel; **S. 113 (Auckland
Prison, New Zealand):** shutterstock/Mati Nitibhon; **S. 121 (Sunnyvale,
California):** shutterstock/Andrew Zarivny.